VETERINARY
MEDICAL SCHOOL
Admission Requirements

in the

United States and Canada

VMSAR

VETERINARY
MEDICAL SCHOOL
Admission Requirements
in the
United States and Canada

1995 Edition
for 1996 matriculation

Association of American Veterinary Medical Colleges

Williams & Wilkins
A WAVERLY COMPANY

BALTIMORE • PHILADELPHIA • LONDON • PARIS • BANGKOK
BUENOS AIRES • HONG KONG • MUNICH • SYDNEY • TOKYO • WROCLAW

1996

Copyright © 1996
Association of American Veterinary Medical Colleges

Published 1996
Williams & Wilkins
Rose Tree Corporate Center
Building II, Suite 5025
1400 North Providence Road
Media, Pa 19063-2043 USA

The information in this book has been supplied by the various schools listed and was updated as of July, 1995. Because information, especially tuition and living expenses, is subject to change, nothing included in this book is binding on any veterinary medical school or on the Association of American Veterinary Medical Colleges.

For the most current and complete information regarding costs, official policies, procedures, and other matters, the applicant should contact the particular school directly. All veterinary medical schools are subject to the requirements of federal and state laws prohibiting discrimination on the basis of race, color, religion, gender, age, handicap, and national origin.

Printed in the United States of America

96 97 98 99
1 2 3 4 5 6 7 8 9 10

1/18/01

CONTENTS

Photo Credits

The cover photograph on this edition of *VMSAR* shows a senior veterinary student and his patient on the lawn of the veterinary teaching hospital at Colorado State University College of Veterinary Medicine at Fort Collins.

The student is shown filling out paperwork to prepare his case for grand rounds. To complete a case for presentation, information in the files must be complete and include all test results and costs.

This photograph is reproduced through the courtesy of Colorado State University College of Veterinary Medicine, Jenger Smith is the photographer.

Black and white photographs in the text were supplied by Purdue University School of Veterinary Medicine and The Ohio State University College of Veterinary Medicine. Photographs on pages 24, 78, and 108 are reproduced through the courtesy of the Purdue Medical Illustration Department.

Submissions from the medical photography staff at The Ohio State College of Veterinary Medicine are reprinted with permission on pages viii, 7, 34, 56, 88, 114, 118, and 137. John J. Swartz and John Jewett are the photographers.

Veterinary Medical Colleges Application Service (VMCAS)

The Veterinary Medical Colleges Application Service has been established by the Association of American Veterinary Medical Colleges for applicants wishing to apply to colleges of veterinary medicine in the United States. VMCAS is a centralized application service, which provides for the collection, processing, verification, and distribution of applicant data to the participating colleges for their use in the applicant selection process. This service is a data-processing component of the admissions cycle only; it is in no way a part of the decision-making process, which is the prerogative of the admissions committees at the various colleges of veterinary medicine.

Application packets are available in July. Completed applications should be submitted to VMCAS no earlier than September 1 of any given year and no later than the earliest deadline indicated by each of the participating colleges to which the applicant wishes to apply.

Each student is eligible to apply to two institutions, for a total fee of $130.00. A fee of $20.00 is charged for each additional institution.

Application deadlines, prerequisite courses, and other aspects of the selection process differ from college to college. Applicants must pay particular attention to the information and instructions included in the application packet for each of the participating colleges. Application packets are available from each of the colleges listed here or from the Association of American Veterinary Medical Colleges (AAVMC), 1101 Vermont Avenue NW, Suite 710, Washington, DC 20005-3521.

The following colleges require that **all** applicants submit their applications through VMCAS:

University of California-Davis	Oregon State University
University of Florida	University of Pennsylvania
Michigan State University	Purdue University
University of Minnesota	University of Tennessee
Mississippi State University	Texas A & M University
North Carolina State University	Washington State University
Oklahoma State University	University of Wisconsin

A few colleges require only applicants who are considered nonresidents to use the service. Resident applicants are not required to use the service and should contact theses colleges directly for the appropriate application materials. Colleges requiring nonresidents to apply through VMCAS include:

Auburn University	Louisiana State University
University of Georgia	Virginia-Maryland Regional College

The service is **optional** for those nonresident applicants who wish to apply to the following colleges. Resident applicants should not use the service and must contact these colleges directly for the appropriate application materials. Colleges with the nonresident option are:

Cornell University

University of Illinois

Iowa State University

Kansas State University

All other colleges require students to contact them directly to request information about their application process. Students wishing to apply to the following colleges must contact them directly:

UNITED STATES

Colorado State University

University of Missouri

Ohio State University

Tufts University

Tuskegee University

CANADA

University of Guelph

Université de Montréal

University of Prince Edward Island

University of Saskatchewan

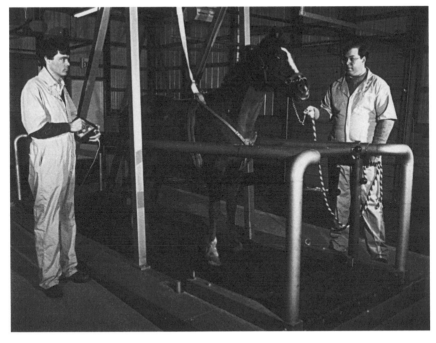

Veterinarians monitor horse's response during an exercise physiology exam at The Ohio State University College of Veterinary Medicine.

PHOTO BY JOHN JEWETT

Veterinary Medicine: Choices and Challenges

Considered from the perspective of comparative medicine, veterinarians help animals and people live longer, healthier lives. They serve society by preventing and treating animal disease, improving the quality of the environment, ensuring the safety of food, controlling diseases transmitted from animals, and advancing medical knowledge. The Doctor of Veterinary Medicine degree can lead to diverse career opportunities and different lifestyles—from a solo mixed animal practice in a rural area to a teaching or research position at an urban university, medical center, or industrial laboratory. The majority of veterinarians in the United States are in private practice, although significant numbers are involved in preventive medicine, regulatory veterinary medicine, military veterinary medicine, laboratory animal medicine, research and development in industry, and teaching and research in a variety of basic science and clinical disciplines.

License to Practice

The DVM (or VMD) degree is awarded after 4 years of successful study at an accredited college of veterinary medicine. Graduate veterinarians are eligible to apply for a license to practice. Licensing is controlled by states and provinces, each of which has established rules and procedures for legal practice within its own jurisdiction. All require satisfactory completion of the national board examination, and most have other requirements, including additional tests and interviews.

Specialization

Graduate veterinarians may choose to become specialists in a clinical area or to work with particular species. The first step on the path toward specialization is usually an internship.

Internship

Internships are 1-year programs in either small or large animal medicine and surgery. The most prestigious internship programs are at veterinary medical colleges or at very large private veterinary hospitals with board-certified veterinarians on staff. Since internships are usually at large referral centers, interns are exposed to a larger number of challenging cases than they would be likely to see in a smaller private practice.

Veterinary students in their senior year and veterinary graduates apply for internships through a matching program. Internship applicants and training hospitals rank each other in order of preference, and a computerized system matches each applicant with the highest-ranking teaching hospital that ranked the applicant. Academic performance in the veterinary professional curriculum, as well as recommendations from veterinary school faculty, are considered in the ranking of internship applicants.

Most veterinary interns in the United States receive a nominal salary, and their educational debts, if any, may be postponed in some governmentally subsidized loan programs. Veterinarians can often command a higher starting salary in private practice after completion of an internship. Also, an internship is the next step, after receiving the DVM degree, toward residency and board certification.

Residency Training

Veterinarians who complete internships or who have 2 years of private practice experience are eligible to apply for residency programs. Residency training is more specialized than an internship. Currently, residency training is available in internal medicine, surgery, cardiology, dermatology, ophthalmology, exotic small animal medicine, pathology, neurology, radiology, anesthesiology, and oncology. The programs take 2 to 3 years to complete, depending on the nature of the specialty. Successful completion of a residency is required for certification by any of the veterinary medical specialty boards. Some residencies combine research and graduate study to lead to a master's degree.

Board Certification

Veterinary board certification and diplomate status are available for 20 specialties: anesthesiology, animal behavior, clinical pharmacology, dentistry, dermatology, emergency and critical care, internal medicine, laboratory animal medicine, microbiology, nutrition, ophthalmology, pathology, poultry medicine, private practice, preventive medicine, radiology, surgery, theriogenology (reproduction), toxicology, and zoological medicine.

Private Practice

Most veterinarians perform clinical work in private practice, either as owner of a solo practice or, increasingly, as a partner or associate in a group practice. The most recent figures on the distribution of practitioners by type of practice indicate that approximately 50% are in small animal practice, approximately 25% are in mixed animal practice, and fewer than 10% are engaged exclusively in large animal practice. Small animal practitioners work primarily with dogs and cats but are seeing a growing number of pet birds and exotic animals, including reptiles. Practices specializing in large animals often emphasize either horses or cows and work on both a farm-call and an in-clinic basis. Mixed animal practices work with all types of animals. Opportunities exist to treat pigs, sheep, goats, llamas, and even some nondomestic animals. Considering species differences and the fact that most veterinarians are general practitioners dealing with a wide variety of health problems, it becomes apparent that there is great variety in the work of a practicing veterinarian.

Private Industry

There are many opportunities for veterinarians in private industry, particularly in the fields of nutrition and pharmaceuticals. Veterinarians may help develop new products in the animal industry, conduct research for a pharmaceutical company, diagnose disease and drug effects as pathologists, or safeguard the health of laboratory animal colonies. Veterinarians are also employed by zoos and aquariums and may act as consultants to wildlife preservation groups or game farms.

Government Agencies

Federal, state, and local government agencies employ veterinarians to ensure the safety of food and as public health officers. Government employment can involve meat inspection, monitoring animal quarantines, herd health review for diseases transmissible to humans, and the care and maintenance of wildlife within state or federal parks and coastal regions. In the United States and Canada, approximately 1350 veterinarians are primarily involved in either regulatory or preventive medicine.

Military

Currently, approximately 400 veterinarians are employed by the Army Veterinary Corps and as Environmental Health Officers in the Air Force.

Academic Institutions

Academic institutions, primarily veterinary medical colleges and schools of human medicine, employ veterinarians as clinicians, researchers, and teachers. Veterinarians work in all of the basic biomedical sciences, including anatomy, biochemistry, microbiology, parasitology, pathology, pharmacology, physiology, and toxicology, as well as in the various clinical specialties.

New or Unusual Career Opportunities

Over time, the role of the veterinarian in society has changed and new career opportunities have become available. Changes in diet and food production have increased the role of veterinary medicine in the poultry and fish production industries. A veterinarian participated as a member of a space shuttle crew. Veterinarians are working in developing countries to raise new breeds of disease-resistant food animals. During recent years, there has been a growing recognition of the need for high-quality health care for wild animals exhibited in zoos and maintained in breeding programs to preserve endangered species. There is also a potential role for veterinarians in the conservation and management of wildlife populations in their natural environments.

Demography of Veterinary Medicine in the United States

Veterinary medicine has changed dramatically in recent years. The population of active veterinarians in the United States has increased approximately 50% since 1980. In 1980, approximately 90% of veterinarians were men, and 10% were women. The proportion of women in veterinary medicine continues to increase in the 1990s. Approximately 70% of current veterinary students are women. Veterinarians work in every state and territory of the United States; however, more than 26% work in California, Texas, Florida, and New York, and 10% of veterinarians in the nation work in California. Growth in the number of veterinarians has tended to be highest in coastal and southern states.

ALPHABETICAL LISTING OF VETERINARY SCHOOLS

United States

Auburn University	Auburn, Alabama
California, University of	Davis, California
Colorado State University	Fort Collins, Colorado
Cornell University	Ithaca, New York
Florida, University of	Gainesville, Florida
Georgia, University of	Athens, Georgia
Illinois, University of	Urbana, Illinois
Iowa State University	Ames, Iowa
Kansas State University	Manhattan, Kansas
Louisiana State University	Baton Rouge, Louisiana
Michigan State University	East Lansing, Michigan
Minnesota, University of	St. Paul, Minnesota
Mississippi State University	Mississippi State, Mississippi
Missouri, University of	Columbia, Missouri
North Carolina State University	Raleigh, North Carolina
Ohio State University	Columbus, Ohio
Oklahoma State University	Stillwater, Oklahoma
Oregon State University	Corvallis, Oregon
Pennsylvania, University of	Philadelphia, Pennsylvania
Purdue University	West Lafayette, Indiana
Tennessee, University of	Knoxville, Tennessee
Texas A & M University	College Station, Texas
Tufts University	North Grafton, Massachusetts
Tuskegee University	Tuskegee, Alabama
Virginia Polytechnic Institute and State University (Virginia-Maryland Regional)	Blacksburg, Virginia
Washington State University	Pullman, Washington
Wisconsin, University of	Madison, Wisconsin

Canada

Guelph, University of	Guelph, Ontario
Montréal, Université de	Montréal, Québec
Prince Edward Island, University of	Charlottetown, Prince Edward Island
Saskatchewan, University of	Saskatoon, Saskatchewan

GEOGRAPHICAL LISTING OF VETERINARY SCHOOLS AND DIRECTORY OF ADMISSIONS OFFICES

United States

Alabama

Committee on Admissions
College of Veterinary Medicine
217 Goodwin Student Center
Auburn University AL 36849-5517

Tuskegee University
School of Veterinary Medicine
Tuskegee AL 36088

California

Office of the Dean
Student Programs
School of Veterinary Medicine
University of California
Davis CA 95616

Colorado

Office of the Dean
College of Veterinary Medicine
    and Biomedical Sciences
Colorado State University
Fort Collins CO 80523

Florida

Admissions Office
College of Veterinary Medicine
P.O. Box 100125
University of Florida
Gainesville FL 32610-0125

Georgia

College of Veterinary Medicine
The University of Georgia
Athens GA 30602-7372

Illinois

College of Veterinary Medicine
University of Illinois
    at Urbana-Champaign
506 South Wright Street
Urbana IL 61801

Indiana

Student Services Office
School of Veterinary Medicine
1240 Lynn Hall
Purdue University
West Lafayette IN 47907-1240

Iowa

Office of Admissions
Room 100 Alumni Hall
Iowa State University
Ames IA 50011

Kansas

Office of the Associate Dean
College of Veterinary Medicine
Veterinary Medical Center
Kansas State University
Trotter Hall
1700 Denison Ave.
Manhattan KS 66506-5601

Louisiana

Office of Veterinary Student Affairs
School of Veterinary Medicine
Louisiana State University
Baton Rouge LA 70803

Massachusetts

Office of Admissions
School of Veterinary Medicine
Tufts University
200 Westborough Road
North Grafton MA 01536

Michigan

Admissions Office
College of Veterinary Medicine
A-126 East Fee Hall
Michigan State University
East Lansing MI 48824-1316

Minnesota

Office of Student Affairs
  and Admission
College of Veterinary Medicine
University of Minnesota
460 Veterinary Teaching Hospital
1365 Gortner Avenue
St. Paul MN 55108

Mississippi

College of Veterinary Medicine
Mississippi State University
P.O. Box 9825
Mississippi State MS 39762

Missouri

Office of Academic Affairs
College of Veterinary Medicine
W203 Veterinary Medicine Building
University of Missouri-Columbia
Columbia MO 65211

New York

Office of Admissions
S1-006 Schurman Hall
College of Veterinary Medicine
Cornell University
Ithaca NY 14853-6401

North Carolina

Office of Admissions
College of Veterinary Medicine
4700 Hillsborough Street
Box 8401
North Carolina State University
Raleigh NC 27606

Ohio

Chairperson, Admissions Committee
College of Veterinary Medicine
0004 Veterinary Hospital
601 Tharp Street
Ohio State University
Columbus OH 43210-1089

Oklahoma

Coordinator of Admissions
College of Veterinary Medicine
Stillwater OK 74078-0353

Oregon

Office of the Dean
200 Magruder Hall
College of Veterinary Medicine
Oregon State University
Corvallis OR 97331-4801

Pennsylvania

Admissions Office
School of Veterinary Medicine
University of Pennsylvania
3800 Spruce Street
Philadelphia PA 19104-6044

Tennessee

Office of the Associate Dean
College of Veterinary Medicine
University of Tennessee
P.O. Box 1071
Knoxville TN 37901-1071

Texas

Office of the Dean
College of Veterinary Medicine
Texas A & M University
College Station TX 77843-4461

Virginia

Admissions Coordinator
Virginia-Maryland Regional College
  of Veterinary Medicine
Virginia Polytechnic Institute
  and State University
Blacksburg VA 24061-0443

Washington

Office of Student Services
College of Veterinary Medicine
Washington State University
Pullman WA 99164-7012

Wisconsin

Office of Academic Affairs
School of Veterinary Medicine
University of Wisconsin-Madison
2015 Linden Drive West
Madison WI 53706

Canada

Ontario

Admissions, Office of the Registrar
University Centre, Level 3
University of Guelph
Guelph, Ontario N1G 2W1

Montréal

Bureau des Admissions
Université de Montréal
C.P. 6205
Succursale A
Montréal Québec H3C 3T5

Prince Edward Island

University of Prince Edward Island
Atlantic Veterinary College
Registrar's Office
550 University Avenue
Charlottetown, PEI C1A 4P3

Saskatchewan

Admissions Office
Western College of Veterinary
  Medicine
University of Saskatchewan
52 Campus Drive
Saskatoon, Saskatchewan 57N 5B4

LISTING OF CONTRACTING STATES AND PROVINCES

All Canadian provinces and twenty states in the United States that do not have a veterinary school contract with one or more schools to provide access to veterinary medical education for their residents. The state or province, working through the contracting agency, usually agrees to pay a fee to help cover the cost of education for a certain number of places in each entering class. Residents from the contract states then compete with each other for those positions.

Some states contract with more than one school. For example, Arkansas contracts with five veterinary schools and North Dakota has contracts with seven schools. Four states (Connecticut, Delaware, Maine, and Vermont) and the District of Columbia presently have no contracts, so all candidates from these places apply "at large" (nonresident/noncontract) to veterinary schools of their choice.

The educational agreements between contracting agencies and veterinary schools differ. Under some contract arrangements, students pay in-state tuition; in others, they pay nonresident tuition. Some contract states require students to repay all or part of the subsidy that the state provided; others require veterinary graduates to return to practice in the state for a period of time. Applicants should be aware of their obligation to the state before agreeing to participate in a contract program.

Following is a list of states and provinces that have educational agreements with schools of veterinary medicine.

States

Alaska

Contracts through WICHE* with University of California, Colorado State University, Kansas State University, and WOI** program.

Arizona

Contracts through WICHE* with University of California, Colorado State University, and WOI** program.

Arkansas

Contracts in past with Tuskegee University, Louisiana State University, Mississippi State University, University of Missouri, and Oklahoma State University. Contracts not all completed at time of printing; may be some changes.

---

* WICHE = Western Interstate Commission for Higher Education (offices in Boulder, Colorado)

** WOI = Washington-Oregon-Idaho Regional Program

5

Georgia

Contracts with Tuskegee University, in addition to having a school in the state.

Hawaii

Contracts through WICHE* with University of California, Colorado State University, and the WOI** program.

Idaho

Contracts with Washington State University as a part of WOI** program.

Kentucky

Contracts with Auburn University and Tuskegee University.

Montana

Contracts with University of California, Colorado State University, and Washington State University.

Nebraska

Contracts with Kansas State University.

Nevada

Contracts through WICHE* with University of California, Colorado State University, and WOI** program.

New Hampshire

Contracts with Cornell University and Tufts University.

New Jersey

Contracts with Cornell University, University of Pennsylvania, Ohio State University, and Tuskegee University.

New Mexico

Contracts through WICHE* with University of California, Colorado State University, Tufts University, and the WOI** program.

North Dakota

Contracts through WICHE* with Iowa State University and the University of Minnesota.

Puerto Rico

Contracts with Cornell University, Kansas State University, Louisiana State University, Ohio State University, University of Pennsylvania, and Tuskegee University.

Rhode Island

Contracts with Tufts University.

South Carolina

Contracts with University of Georgia and Tuskegee University.

South Dakota

Reciprocity with University of Minnesota. Contracts with Iowa State University.

Utah

Contracts through WICHE* with University of California, Colorado State University, and the WOI** program.

West Virginia

Contracts with University of Georgia, Ohio State University, and Tuskegee University.

Wyoming

Contracts with University of California, Colorado State University, Kansas State University, and Washington State University.

Provinces

Alberta

Contracts with University of Saskatchewan.

British Columbia

Contracts with University of Saskatchewan.

Manitoba

Contracts with University of Saskatchewan.

New Brunswick

Contracts with Atlantic Veterinary College at the University of Prince Edward Island.

Newfoundland

Contracts with Atlantic Veterinary College at the University of Prince Edward Island.

Northwest Territory

Contracts with University of Saskatchewan.

Nova Scotia

Contracts with Atlantic Veterinary College at the University of Prince Edward Island.

Yukon Territory

Contracts with University of Saskatchewan.

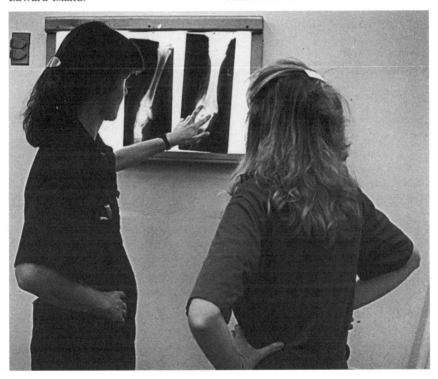

For a cow under treatment, senior veterinary students are examining a radiograph of the cow's leg fracture in the large animal facility at The Ohio State University College of Veterinary Medicine.

PHOTO BY JOHN J. SWARTZ

Directory of Contracting States Agencies

Students from states that contract with specific schools must have their residency certified by the contracting agency from that state in order to participate in the contract program.

Obligations on the student's part in terms of payback or work requirements vary widely from state to state.

For information on the contract program that applies to you, write to the contract representative from your state, which is listed below.

Alabama

Alabama Commission on Higher
   Education, Suite 221
One Court Square
Montgomery, AL 36104-3584

Alaska

Certifying Officer for Alaska
WICHE Student Exchange Program
Alaska Commission on Postsecondary
   Education
3030 Vintage Boulevard
Juneau AK 99801-7109

Arizona

Certifying Officer for Arizona
WICHE Student Exchange Program
Arizona Board of Regents
2020 North Central, Suite 253
Phoenix AZ 85004

Arkansas

Dr. Diane Suitt Guilleland, Director
Arkansas Department of Higher
   Education
114 East Capitol Avenue
Little Rock AR 72201-3818

Georgia

Assistant Executive Secretary
Board of Regents of the University
   System of Georgia
244 Washington Street, S.W.
Atlanta GA 30334

Hawaii

Certifying Officer for Hawaii
WICHE Student Exchange Program
Postsecondary Education Commission
2444 Dole St., Bachman Hall
Honolulu HI 96822

Idaho

(WOI Regional Program)
Office of Student Services
Washington State University
Pullman WA 99164-7012
Kathleen Potter
Director of WOI Admissions

Kentucky

Deputy Executive Director,
   Academic Affairs
Council on Higher Education
1050 U.S. 27 South, Suite 101
Frankfort KY 40601-4395
(502) 564-3553

8

Montana

Certifying Officer for Montana
WICHE Student Exchange Program
2500 Broadway
Helena, MT 59620-3101

Nebraska

Dr. Jack Schmitz, DVM Coordinator
Dept. of Veterinary and Biomedical
  Sciences
University of Nebraska-Lincoln
Lincoln NE 68583-0905

Nevada

Certifying Officer for Nevada
WICHE Student Exchange Program
2601 Enterprise Road
Reno NV 89512

New Hampshire

James Busselle
Executive Director
Postsecondary Education Commission
2 Industrial Park Drive
Concord NH 03301-8512

New Jersey

Eugene Hutchins
Accounting Office
State of New Jersey
20 West State Street
CN 542
Trenton NJ 08625

New Mexico

Certifying Officer for New Mexico
WICHE Student Exchange Program
The University of New Mexico
Student Services Center, Room 261
Albuquerque NM 87131

North Dakota

Certifying Officer for North Dakota
WICHE Student Exchange Program
North Dakota University System
Capitol Building, 10th Floor
600 East Blvd. Avenue
Bismarck ND 58505-0230

or

Dr. M. H. Smith
Dept. of Veterinary and
  Microbiological Sciences
North Dakota State University
Fargo ND 58105

Puerto Rico

Dr. Maria E. Cora-Block
Dean of Students
UPR Medical Sciences Campus
P.O. Box 365067
San Juan PR 00936-5067

Rhode Island

Rhode Island Higher Education
  Assistance Authority
Linda Daigle, Accounting Dept.
560 Jefferson Boulevard
Warwick RI 02886

South Carolina

Associate Commissioner for
  Academic Affairs
South Carolina Commission on
  Higher Education
1333 Main Street, Suite 200
Columbia SC 29201

South Dakota

South Dakota Board of Regents
Veterinary Tuition Assistance
  Program
207 East Capitol Avenue
Pierre SD 57501-3159

Utah

Certifying Officer for Utah
WICHE Student Exchange Program
#3 Triad Center
Suite 550
Salt Lake City UT 84180-1205

West Virginia

Dr. Robert Dailey, Interim Chair
College of Agriculture and Forestry
Division of Animal and Veterinary
    Science
West Virginia University
Box 6108
Morgantown WV 26506-6108

or

Dr. Joseph W. Corder, Jr.
Coordinator, Academic Contract
    Programs
State College and University Systems
    of West Virginia
1018 Kanawha Boulevard-East
Suite 700
Charleston WV 25301

Wyoming

Certifying Officer for Wyoming
WICHE Student Exchange Program
University Station, Box 3432
Laramie WY 82071-3432

Listing of Schools Accepting "At Large" Applications (Nonresident/Noncontract)

United States	Number of Positions Available
Auburn University	Ten positions; U.S. citizens only.
University of California	Limited number.
Colorado State University	15-20 positions; international applicants considered.
Cornell University	Varies, between 15-18 positions available; international applicants considered.
University of Florida	Not more than 15% of entering class (13 in 1995).
University of Georgia	Total to ten spaces.
University of Illinois	20-30 are offered admission. U. of I. offers 20-30 nonresident positions initially and has no alternate list for nonresidents. University of Illinois targets 15 nonresidents; however, *all* could enroll.
Iowa State University	25 spaces available, plus unfilled contract positions; international applicants considered.
Kansas State University	Approximately 15%-20% of class, plus unfilled contract positions (22 in 1994); priority to U.S. citizens.
Louisiana State University	Limited number (ten in 1995).
Michigan State University	Not more than 20%-25% of entering class (20 in 1995).

University of Minnesota	Not more than 20% of entering class (15 in 1995).
Mississippi State University	19 spaces.
University of Missouri	Eight spaces were available in 1995; priority given to applicants from states without a veterinary school.
North Carolina State University	12 spaces.
Ohio State University	15–30 positions.
Oklahoma State University	May accept up to 14 first-time nonresident students (policy subject to change).
Oregon State University	Limited number. No minimum. Maximum of eight.
University of Pennsylvania	Total 45–50 spaces, including foreign applicants.
Purdue University	Approximately 20 spaces available; international applicants will be considered.
University of Tennessee	Maximum of 15–20 positions; Tennessee residents given preference.
Texas A & M University	Limited number (seven in 1995).
Tufts University	35–40 positions.
Tuskegee University	Total 40–45 "at large" spaces.
Virginia-Maryland Regional College of Veterinary Medicine	Up to ten positions.
Washington State University	Limited number (five in 1995).
University of Wisconsin	10–20 nonresident positions (ten in 1995).

Canada

University of Prince Edward Island	Nine positions for international applicants.

Policies on Advanced Standing

Transfers are permitted to most colleges of veterinary medicine in the United States under specified conditions. Typical requirements are a vacancy in the class, completion of all prerequisite requirements, and compatible curricula. Following is a listing of schools and some of the circumstances under which they will consider a transfer from another veterinary college with advanced standing. More detailed information may be obtained by writing to individual schools.

University of California

1. An opening must exist in the second- or third-year class.
2. The applicant must have completed equivalent course work to that of students in the class to which that person seeks admission.
3. The applicant must meet the minimum academic requirements for admission as stated in the Announcement of the School of Veterinary Medicine.
4. Priority is given to California residents. It is usually not possible to determine if a position will be available until after July 1 in any given year. No positions available for the 1996–97 academic year.

Colorado State University

Students from schools of veterinary medicine accredited by the A.V.M.A. will be considered on an individual and space-available basis.

University of Florida

1. Students with advanced standing are rarely considered for admission to second-year class on the basis of exceptional personal circumstances.
2. Student must be enrolled in an A.V.M.A.-accredited college.
3. Student must meet all prerequisites for admission as a first-year student (including GRE scores).
4. The curricula of the two schools must be sufficiently alike to allow a student to enter second-year class without deficiencies in academic background.
5. Applicant must *not* have been denied admission to the University of Florida College of Veterinary Medicine as a first-year student.
6. Applicants must have a letter approving transfer from their Dean or Associate Dean.

The University of Georgia

1. Must be a resident of the U.S., with priority given to Georgia residents, followed by contract state residents, then southeast regional residents, and all citizens.
2. Applicants are rarely considered for entry into the second year.

3. Applicants from United States veterinary schools must demonstrate a hardship documented by the dean of the school in which the applicant is currently enrolled.
4. All selection criteria for regular applicants apply to transfer applicants.

University of Illinois

On a limited basis, admission of students with advanced standing from other accredited U.S. veterinary schools will be considered on a case-by-case review.

Iowa State University

1. The applicant must have had essentially the same preveterinary course work as required of Iowa State students.
2. The applicant must have completed the equivalent of all courses required of Iowa State University veterinary students beginning the academic term the applicant seeks to enter. Only credits earned at an A.V.M.A.-accredited college of veterinary medicine will be considered for credit.
3. The applicant must have been in good standing throughout his or her entire period of enrollment in the school(s) of veterinary medicine in which the student is, or has been, enrolled. A letter to that effect from the dean(s) of the school(s) is required.
4. Space must be available.

Kansas State University

1. Acceptance of students for advanced standing is on recommendation of the Admissions Committee on a space-available basis.
2. Applicant must meet all preprofessional entrance criteria and have satisfactory standing at the original institution; must also be able to begin at Kansas State University in at least the first semester of the second year.
3. Priority is given to United States citizens, especially Kansas residents and residents of contract states.
4. A.V.M.A. accreditation status of institution of origin is an important criterion.

Louisiana State University

Applicants must have successfully completed all previous professional courses in an A.V.M.A.-accredited college or school of veterinary medicine. The request for transfer and supporting documents are reviewed by the Committee on Admissions. After review the committee forwards a recommendation to the dean for approval or denial of the transfer request.

Michigan State University

1. Admission consideration is offered only to those current matriculants in professional veterinary curricula who believe that there are extenuating circumstances that would precipitate significant undue hardship if they continue at their current institution.
2. Applicants must also demonstrate quality academic performance throughout their professional school enrollment.
3. Priority is given to Michigan residents.

University of Minnesota

1. Transfers are not allowed to any specific requested year or quarter. The Committee will place each applicant in the year or quarter of the curriculum deemed appropriate after analysis of equivalency of the required courses involved.
2. No academic work or standing will be accepted from D.V.M. curricula other than those deemed accredited ("AVMA-accredited") or approved ("AVMA-approved") by the American Veterinary Medical Association.
3. All applicants must be U.S. or Canadian citizens, be holders of permanent resident alien visas, or have achieved landed immigrant status.
4. All applicants are required to have finished at least one full academic year at the institution from which transfer is requested and must be in good academic standing at the time of discontinuance according to written verification from the Associate Dean for Academic Affairs or Dean of that institution.
5. All applicants must document that not more than two calendar years have elapsed between discontinuance and application to our D.V.M. program.
6. All applicants must have achieved a cumulative GPA of 3.0 (of 4.0) for the required courses at the initial institution.
7. All applicants must present suitable transcripts and course summary descriptions of all courses taken. These must be carried to the appropriate course coordinator in our curriculum, and each coordinator must certify in writing that the transfer courses satisfy our curricular specifications, according to comparative criteria determined by each coordinator in discussion with the petitioner. The applicant is responsible for preparing a standard University of Minnesota Petition Form, obtaining the course instructor's dated signature, and returning it to the Office for Student Affairs and Admission. If equivalency is not certified, the course must be taken in our curriculum prior to the transfer to a specific veterinary class year.

Mississippi State University

The College of Veterinary Medicine accepts a limited number of transfer students from other colleges of veterinary medicine in order to maintain a stable class size. Transfer positions are filled on a competitive basis.

Students interested in transferring into the professional program should send a letter of intent and an official transcript from their current college of veterinary medicine to: *Academic Program Director, College of Veterinary Medicine, P.O. Box 9825, Mississippi State MS 39762*. Upon receipt of this material, academic program personnel will analyze the transcript, determine the appropriate entry point into the professional curriculum, and determine whether any positions are available for that class in the program. If positions are available, candidates will be invited to interview for a position in the class. Candidates cannot transfer into the program beyond the first semester of the third year of the curriculum. Guidelines for transfer applicants:

1. Transfer applicants must attend an interview at the College of Veterinary Medicine to be eligible for admission.

2. Transfer applicants must submit complete transcripts of all D.V.M. course work.
3. Transfers are limited to the first two years of the curriculum. No student can transfer into the curriculum beyond the start of the third year of the professional program.
4. Candidates must demonstrate quality academic performance and professional behavior to be considered for transfer. Transfer applicants who have failed one or more courses at another college of veterinary medicine will not be considered for admission. Transfer applicants who have been dismissed for academic or other reasons from any other college of veterinary medicine will not be considered for admission.
5. To initiate transfer, candidates must submit a formal letter of application, stating reasons for transfer, and an official transcript from their professional program.

University of Missouri

1. Must be a vacancy in the class.
2. Will consider students who are U.S. citizens or holders of permanent alien visas and who have finished at least two years in a college of veterinary medicine that is AVMA accredited or approved.
3. Students must be in good academic standing, and letters of reference from the Dean's Office and at least two faculty members of the present college are required.

North Carolina State University

1. Must be a vacancy in the class.
2. Consideration by the admission committee on an individual basis.
3. Curricula must be compatible.
4. Should meet same requirements as first-year applicants.
5. Support letter required from the Dean's office.

Ohio State University

1. An opening must exist.
2. Student must be enrolled in an A.V.M.A.-accredited college.
3. The curricula of the two schools must be sufficiently alike to allow the student to enter a class without deficiencies in his or her academic background.
4. Student must be in good academic standing in present college and have a supporting letter from the Dean of Student and Academic Affairs to this effect.
5. Each request for transfer is considered on an individual basis, taking into account personal hardship, family situations, etc.
6. Must meet same prerequisite requirements as first-year applicants.

Oklahoma State University

1. A student will normally enter at the beginning of the fall semester, second year, regardless of his/her standing at the school from which he/she is transferring.
2. A student may be accepted only if a vacancy exists in the second-year class, fall semester.

3. Preference will be given to students from schools/colleges accredited by the A.V.M.A. Council on Education.
4. Application deadline is April 15, with all requirements having been met prior to entry date.
5. Applications accepted only from students from institutions that are accredited by an authentic accrediting agency.

Oregon State University

Admission of students with advanced standing is considered only in very specific and unique circumstances and each case is considered on an individual basis.

University of Pennsylvania

1. An opening must exist.
2. Admission with Advanced Standing (AAS) is considered only from institutions that are accredited by the A.V.M.A.
3. Student must initiate the process at his/her own institution. The Dean of Student Affairs at the college from which the student wants to transfer must understand the student's need for AAS and endorse it. The usual reasons endorsed are either medical or the desire to move nearer one's spouse.
4. If the Dean of Student Affairs approves, student must send detailed description of all coursework taken to date and simultaneously submit an application to the University of Pennsylvania's admissions committee. If the admissions committee accepts the credentials, they will compare coursework with that of the University of Pennsylvania and determine where in the curriculum the student might be placed.
5. If all criteria are met and space is available, AAS may be granted.
6. University of Pennsylvania cannot award a degree to a student who has completed less than 50% of graduation credits at Penn.

Purdue University

1. Must be a vacancy in the class.
2. Curricula must be compatible.
3. Must be in good academic standing at present college.
4. Must have an acceptable undergraduate record as determined by the Admissions Committee.
5. Admission limited to the first or second year of the program.

Texas A & M University

Students requesting advanced standing must meet the following requirements:
1. Must have completed all previous professional veterinary courses in an A.V.M.A.-accredited college of veterinary medicine.
2. Must have successfully completed the academic term preceding the semester into which student requests admission.
3. Must comply with all requirements for transfer into the University as described in the current TAMU catalog.
4. May request transfer only into the second through seventh semesters of the professional curriculum.

5. At the time of matriculation in the College of Veterinary Medicine at Texas A & M University, the student must certify by letter to the Associate Dean for Academic Programs that he/she has not been convicted of crimes in the period from first enrollment in the college of veterinary medicine from which the student desires transfer until date of matriculation at Texas A & M University.

All students requesting advanced standing into the professional curriculum leading to the D.V.M. degree at Texas A & M University College of Veterinary Medicine are required to:

1. Submit a letter to the Associate Dean for Academic Programs of the College of Veterinary Medicine that specifies:
   a. reason(s) for requesting transfer,
   b. desired date of transfer, and
   c. class and semester of curriculum into which transfer is requested.
2. Provide a letter of character and academic reference (including class ranking) from the Dean of the college of veterinary medicine from which student desires the transfer.
3. Provide two letters of reference from former instructors who are members of the faculty of the college of veterinary medicine from which student desires the transfer.
4. Provide official copies of all academic transcripts.

Tufts University

Applicants from other veterinary schools are welcome. Students with advanced standing are admitted if and when space becomes available in the second or third-year class. The application deadline is June 1 for the following September.

Virginia Polytechnic Institute and State University

1. Must be a Virginia or Maryland resident or a nonresident enrolled in another veterinary school.
2. Advanced standing is allowed only if vacancy exists. Class size cannot exceed 90 students. Must start at beginning of second or third year.
3. Must have a 3.0 GPA in veterinary school attended.
4. Must submit transcripts from all colleges attended and meet minimum GPA requirements for all college work.
5. Must have completed the same preprofessional courses required for first-year admission with a grade of C or higher.
6. Letters from current Dean and two faculty members are required.
7. Petition for advanced standing, with reasons for same, must be received by May 1 of the year in which transfer occurs.

Washington State University

Admission of students with advanced standing is effected only in very specific and unique circumstances and each case is considered on an individual basis.

University of Wisconsin

Accepts applications for transfer. Each applicant will be evaluated using the same selection criteria established for applicants to the first-year class. Applications for admission with advanced standing to the School of Veterinary Medicine will be considered under the following circumstances:

1. Applicant will be considered for admission only if there is space available in the class into which he/she wishes to enter.
2. The applicant must have attended an A.V.M.A.-accredited college of veterinary medicine.
3. Applicant must have passed all professional courses and attained the minimum cumulative GPA required for promotion of students at the University of Wisconsin-Madison School of Veterinary Medicine.
4. Wisconsin residents will be given first consideration for admission if the above criteria have been met.

University of Guelph

Admission with advanced standing from other veterinary schools will be considered provided a vacancy exists and the applicant can fulfill the residence requirements and has a satisfactory academic record.

University of Prince Edward Island

Applicants who have completed all or portions of a veterinary medical program may apply for advanced standing to the second or third year of the D.V.M. program. Applicants for advanced standing must present evidence of educational accomplishments and may be required to satisfactorily pass examinations in all of the courses for which they desire credit. Students admitted with advanced standing must begin the college year in September.

The candidate must file a formal application and may be interviewed by the Selection Committee and possibly other faculty. Places for admission to the college with advanced standing are limited and depend on vacancies.

It is imperative that the Selection Committee have detailed and translated summaries of veterinary medical academic programs and accomplishments for those seeking advanced placement from schools in foreign countries. Advanced standing applications should be on file and completed as early as possible and no later than January 1.

University of Saskatchewan

1. Must have a vacancy.
2. Curricula must be compatible.
3. Residency requirements apply.
4. Seldom is anyone admitted beyond the second year.
5. GRE is required.

Combined D.V.M. Degree with Other Graduate Degree Programs

Excellent career opportunities exist for veterinarians with research expertise. The current need for veterinary medical teachers and researchers encourages schools of veterinary medicine to make programs available which combine the Doctor of Veterinary Medicine (D.V.M.) and Doctor of Philosophy (Ph.D.). Currently, 70% of all the veterinary schools in the United States make some provision for combining or working concurrently on these degrees. The schools listed below offer a brief description of their respective programs. For more information, each school should be contacted directly.

University of California

A student may elect to enroll in a combined D.V.M./M.P.V.M. program (i.e., Doctor of Veterinary Medicine and Master of Preventive Veterinary Medicine degrees) in which the D.V.M. degree will normally be awarded at the end of the fall or winter quarter of the fifth year. The advantage of combining the two programs on a concurrent basis resides in the ability of the student to complete the M.P.V.M. program within six months after normal completion time of the D.V.M. degree, rather than fifteen months as would be the case if taken sequentially.

No formal combined D.V.M. and M.S. or Ph.D. program is available. However, students may work toward the D.V.M. degree and the graduate academic degree as joint majors. Individual joint major programs are established following consultation with the Associate Deans of Student Programs and Academic Programs.

Colorado State University

The program combines advanced study and research in a selected field with training in biomedical and clinical sciences in the professional curriculum. Applicants will choose a research program and advisor during the first two years of the degree program and begin the graduate program during the summer following the second year of their professional program. Graduates will be qualified to join faculties in medical professional schools or universities or to pursue research careers in industry or government agencies in the fields of anatomy, environmental health, microbiology, neurobiology, pathology, physiology, public health, and radiation biology. This program offers an opportunity for a limited number of highly qualified and motivated students to engage in a six- to seven-year educational program leading to both the D.V.M. and M.S. or Ph.D. degrees.

Cornell University

Once accepted into the D.V.M. program, exceptional students may apply to the Graduate School of Cornell University. Students work on the D.V.M. during the academic year and on graduate programs during the summers. At least an extra year after the completion of the D.V.M. is required to complete the graduate degree. Two graduate assistantships a year are reserved for D.V.M./Ph.D. students and are awarded on a competitive basis. The assistantships fund summer work during the D.V.M. program and pay a stipend and graduate tuition after completion of the D.V.M. degree.

University of Illinois

D.V.M./Ph.D. and D.V.M./Law combined programs are available.

Iowa State University

Qualified students may be concurrently enrolled in the professional curriculum leading to the D.V.M. degree and in a graduate program leading to the M.S. or Ph.D. degree after completion of at least 128 semester credits, or their quarter equivalents, in preveterinary and professional curricula. Admission to the concurrent D.V.M.-graduate degree programs is subject to the approval of the Dean of the Graduate College and Dean of the College of Veterinary Medicine.

Kansas State University

Students in the veterinary medicine curriculum who have a B.S. degree may concurrently pursue a Master's degree and apply 12 semester hours of selected D.V.M. courses toward the requirements for the M.S.

University of Minnesota

The College of Veterinary Medicine at the University of Minnesota offers a combined D.V.M./Ph.D. program for a limited number of students admitted to both the D.V.M. program and the Graduate School. This program offers AFW Scholarships to three entering students per year. The scholarship includes in-state tuition and a stipend while enrolled in the veterinary curriculum and a graduate assistantship while in the Graduate School.

Mississippi State University

D.V.M./M.S. and D.V.M./Ph.D. programs are available.

University of Missouri

Students with a baccalaureate degree who are in the professional program may also enroll in a graduate program provided they meet Graduate School criteria for admission. Students must have a B.S. degree to be eligible.

North Carolina State University

The college offers a combined D.V.M./Ph.D. program for a limited number of students admitted to both the College of Veterinary Medicine professional program and the Graduate School. This program is designed to reduce the time required for completion of both degrees. Those who are interested in this program should contact the Director of Graduate Studies at the time they are seeking admission to the veterinary professional program of the college.

Ohio State University

A veterinary medical student with demonstrated proficiency who is registered in the College of Veterinary Medicine of this university and who also wishes to enroll for graduate study may be registered concurrently in the Graduate School if he or she possesses the proper qualifications for admission. The veterinary medical student must have approval of the Dean of the College of Veterinary Medicine for dual registration, which may be obtained through the college's Student Affairs Office, and must obtain admission to the Graduate School through the Director of the Admissions Office. Successful completion of the first year of the veterinary curriculum is required for consideration for admission to the combined degree program.

Oklahoma State University

Basic sciences departments offer Master of Science (M.S.) and Ph.D. degree programs. Dual degree programs are limited to D.V.M./M.S. at present.

Oregon State University

A combined degree program can be available after acceptance into the professional program and in discussion with the person who would serve as a major professor.

University of Pennsylvania

V.M.D./M.B.A., five or six years combined. School of Veterinary Medicine and Wharton School of Business. An application to the Wharton School is required simultaneously.

V.M.D./Ph.D., six or more years to earn a V.M.D. and a Ph.D. in a basic science. The Veterinary Medical Scientist Training Program is supported by the National Institutes of Health, and questions should be directed to Dr. John H. Wolfe, Program Director-VMSTP, School of Veterinary Medicine, University of Pennsylvania, 3800 Spruce St., Philadelphia PA 19104.

Purdue University

A combined DVM/PhD program is offered jointly by the School of Veterinary Medicine and the Graduate School. This program is designed to provide research training to highly qualified and strongly motivated students to pursue academic and research careers in the biomedical sciences. The requirements of both the PhD and DVM programs can be completed in six to seven years. The program is tailored to the background and career goals of the student. Areas of concentration include physiology, pharmacology, toxicology, anatomy, embryology, pathology, immunology, epidemiology, and the interdisciplinary areas of bioengineering, medicinal chemistry, molecular biology, and neurosciences.

Tufts University

D.V.M./M.S., with Tufts University Fletcher School of Law and Diplomacy. Designed to prepare veterinary students who intend to seek international policy-making positions in the provision of veterinary services in areas such as livestock development, wildlife management, and fisheries biology.

D.V.M./M.S., in Applied Biotechnology with Worcester Polytechnic Institute. Designed to prepare veterinary students for careers in biotechnology. In-depth study in microbial genetics, DNA technology, and genetic engineering.

D.V.M./M.S., in Animals and Public Policy with Tufts Center for Animals and Public Policy. Designed to prepare veterinary students for careers where a thorough knowledge of animal welfare issues and history combined with an understanding of underlying attitudes and values toward animals will assist in expanding their role as animal health professionals in the arena of public policy.

D.V.M./M.P.H., with Tufts University School of Medicine. Designed to prepare veterinary students for a career in public health, or to better apply the principles of epidemiology and public health to more traditional forms of practice or research.

D.V.M./Ph.D., with the University of Massachusetts Medical Center and with Tufts' Sackler School for Graduate Biomedical Sciences. The Ph.D. concentrations include biochemistry, cell biology, immunology and virology, molecular genetics and microbiology, neuroscience, pharmacology, and physiology.

Tuskegee University

The dual D.V.M./M.S. program is designed to meet the needs of the advanced veterinary student who desires specialized training at the graduate level. Qualified students may enroll in this program during the summer after their second year of study. Students applying for this program must meet all other graduate admission requirements. The time required to complete this program depends on the student and the complexity of the research program. Students in the dual D.V.M./M.S. program will be permitted to enroll in graduate courses *only* during the summer session.

Virginia Polytechnic Institute and State University

Students with a 3.4 GPA in the preveterinary undergraduate programs may apply for acceptance to our graduate program (D.V.M./M.S. or Ph.D.). If in the professional veterinary college, a GPA of 3.3 in the first or second year is required. Students are registered for the D.V.M. program in regular academic session and register for graduate work in the summer. If funds are available, a limited number of financial aid awards, fellowships, or scholarships may be available for the summer sessions. Graduate programs exist in basic biomedical and clinical sciences.

Washington State University

The program allows concurrent pursuit of D.V.M. and M.S. or Ph.D. There is no stipulation as to the graduate major. Duplicate credit is allowed for both professional degree and graduate degree to the extent of 11 semester credit hours in an M.S. program and 15 semester credit hours in a Ph.D. program. An extension of time from one to four years beyond the D.V.M. degree is necessary for full completion of both degrees.

University of Wisconsin

No formal combined D.V.M. and M.S. or Ph.D. program is available. The student may work toward the D.V.M. degree and a graduate degree as joint majors. As a joint major the D.V.M. student could take graduate course work and participate in research during the four-year D.V.M. program. Typically, additional work is necessary to complete the graduate degree after the D.V.M. degree is awarded. A formal combined program may be available in the future. Interested applicants should contact the Associate Dean of Academic Affairs.

Senior students at Purdue's Veterinary Medical Teaching Hospital prep these feline patients to undergo a cystocentesis procedure.

PROGRAMS FOR MINORITY OR DISADVANTAGED STUDENTS

Veterinary medicine, like all professions, needs individuals from many different backgrounds to serve the needs of an increasingly diverse society. The colleges of veterinary medicine are committed to increasing the racial and ethnic diversity of their student populations.

Many schools have programs designed to facilitate entry into and retention by veterinary programs nationwide. These programs are directed at several levels, from high school students to the student who has already been accepted by a veterinary college. Most of these programs will accept students from every state, regardless of which school(s) an individual might eventually apply to or attend.

Following is an alphabetical list of schools by state and a short explanation of their programs:

Auburn University College of Veterinary Medicine

Program: SUMMER LABORATORY EXPERIENCES FOR HIGH SCHOOL STUDENTS

Description: students who have demonstrated an interest in the biological or health sciences will spend eight weeks working in the laboratory of a senior research scientist. Whenever possible, students will design and conduct an experiment, and present the results to students and faculty during an exit seminar. Orientation sessions will provide the student with the basics of laboratory safety and an introduction to sterile technique. An enrichment program will provide information on career-related opportunities and cultural programs.

Eligibility: minority high school students who have completed the junior or senior year with strong grades in science and recommendations from their teachers will be considered.

Contact person: Dr. Kenneth Nusbaum, Coordinator of Recruiting, College of Veterinary Medicine, Auburn University, AL 36849-5519, telephone: (334) 844-2693; fax: (334) 844-2652.

Sponsorship: National Institutes of Health, National Center for Research Resources.

University of California

Program: SUMMER ENRICHMENT PROGRAM (SEP) (funded through summer 1995)

Description: a seven-week summer residential program. The purpose of this program is to increase the academic preparedness of ethnic minority disadvantaged students through science-based learning skills development, clinical education, individual advising, and student development.

Eligibility: junior, senior, or postbaccalaureate student. Educationally and/or economically disadvantaged. Must have a cumulative undergraduate and required science GPA of 2.50 and demonstrated interest in veterinary medicine.

Program dates: begins last week of June and ends second week in August.

Contact person: Ms. Valentine Garcia, School of Veterinary Medicine, University of California-Davis, Davis CA 95616-8731; telephone: (916) 752-1383.

Sponsorship: Health Careers Opportunity Program.

Colorado State University

Program: Vet Start

Description: a seven-year undergraduate and professional program for diverse and disadvantaged students who come to Colorado State from high school or with less than 15 semester credits of college coursework. Undergraduate and professional program in-state tuition and fee scholarships are provided, and admission to the professional veterinary medical program is guaranteed upon successful completion of the undergraduate requirements. Mentoring, support services, and summer jobs are also provided.

Eligibility: students who are ethnically diverse or who come from a disadvantaged background (cultural, social, or economical). Students must be residents of Colorado or one of the WICHE states (AK, AZ, HI, ND, NM, NV, UT, or WY), and must be a high school graduate with less than 15 semester credits of college coursework. Selection is competitive.

Program dates: begins fall semester; applications available January 1; application deadline April 15.

Contact person: Dr. Sherry McConnell, College of Veterinary Medicine & Biomedical Sciences, W102 Anatomy, Colorado State University, Fort Collins, CO 80523; telephone: (970) 491-7052.

Sponsorship: College of Veterinary Medicine & Biomedical Sciences, Colorado State University and USDA.

Cornell University

Program: REGENTS PROFESSIONAL OPPORTUNITIES SCHOLARSHIPS

Description: a financial assistance program for New York residents who are underrepresented minorities. Must be New York resident and must agree to work in New York for a time after graduation.

Contact person: Gloria Crissey, Director of Financial Aid, College of Veterinary Medicine, Cornell University, S1 006 Schurman Hall, Ithaca NY 14853-6401.

Program: STATE UNIVERSITY OF NEW YORK GRADUATE UNDERREPRESENTED MINORITY FELLOWSHIPS

Description: all matriculating underrepresented minorities are eligible (not restricted by state residency).

Contact person: Gloria Crissey, Director of Financial Aid, College of Veterinary Medicine, Cornell University, S1 006 Schurman Hall, Ithaca NY 14853-6401.

University of Florida

Program: POSTBACCALAUREATE PROGRAM

Description: a year-round individually tailored academic and veterinary experience to enrich the student's background and strengthen his/her admissibility to the professional veterinary medicine curriculum.

Eligibility: students who have completed an undergraduate degree and show potential for admission to the professional program.

Contact person: Dr. L. F. Archbald, Coordinator of Minority Programs, College of Veterinary Medicine, University of Florida, Gainesville FL 32610; telephone: (904) 392-4700, ext. 5600.

University of Illinois

Program: MINORITY HIGH SCHOOL RESEARCH APPRENTICESHIP PROGRAM (RAP)

Description: RAP is a six-week residential program which provides underrepresented minority students with an opportunity to work in research laboratories under the guidance of faculty members in the College of Veterinary Medicine. Students contribute to the ongoing research activities of their mentor and attend career awareness seminars and computer or mathematics classes. Students receive an hourly stipend for their work, and housing is provided in a University residence hall.

Eligibility: African-American, Hispanic, and Native American juniors and seniors in high school are eligible to apply if they rank in the upper third of their class and demonstrate an interest in pursuing a career in science after completing college. Selection will be based on academic performance, evidence of interest in the health sciences, and a letter of recommendation from a teacher or counselor.

Program dates: Late June through July (6 weeks).

Contact person: Associate Dean for Academic and Student Affairs, University of Illinois, College of Veterinary Medicine, 2001 South Lincoln, 2271G VMBSB, Urbana IL 61801; telephone: (217) 333-1192.

Sponsorship: National Institutes of Health and the U.S. Department of Agriculture.

Program: NONTRADITIONAL STUDENT ASSESSMENT PROGRAM (NSAP)

Description: NSAP is an admissions and retention program for socially, culturally, or economically disadvantaged students seeking admission to veterinary school. An evaluation process is used in which noncognitive factors are considered in addition to the standard selection criteria. Applicants must meet the minimum academic requirements of the College for consideration. Application material is sent to all applicants so that those who think they qualify and wish to apply may submit the required information.

Louisiana State University

Program: SUMMER RESEARCH APPRENTICESHIP PROGRAM

Description: this is a ten-week program designed to provide junior and senior minority high school students with a meaningful experience in a research laboratory setting. The students are assigned to a mentor and are paid minimum wage. Selection is competitive.

Eligibility: high school juniors and seniors. One to five students are selected to participate.

Program dates: 10 weeks from the first week in June to August.

Contact person: Earl P. Godfrey, Recruiter/Counselor, Office of Veterinary Student Affairs, Louisiana State University, Baton Rouge LA 70803; telephone: (504) 346-3220.

Michigan State University

Program: VETWARD BOUND PROGRAM

Description: Vetward Bound offers five levels of programming, each with is own eligibility requirements. Students from high school through prematriculants into the professional program are provided a review of basic science content, research experience, preparation for the MCAT, veterinary experience, study strategy development, and field experiences. Placement in a specific level is determined by program staff and is based on educational background.

Eligibility: high school through prematriculants into the professional degree program.

Program dates: June through August for five to ten weeks, depending on the specific program content.

Contact person: Vetward Bound Coordinator, A-136 East Fee Hall, College of Veterinary Medicine, Michigan State University, East Lansing MI 48824–1316; telephone (517) 355-6521.

University of Minnesota

Program: HIGH SCHOOL RESEARCH APPRENTICE PROGRAM

Description: an eight-week program to give junior and senior high school students the opportunity to discover what takes place in a research laboratory. Students work full-time with volunteer faculty researchers from the health and biological sciences. Students are paid minimum wage.

Eligibility: junior and senior high school students.

Program dates: mid-June through mid-August

Contact person: Larry Bjorklund, Director, Student Affairs, College of Veterinary Medicine, University of Minnesota, 1365 Gortner Avenue, St. Paul MN 55108; telephone: (612) 624-4747.

Sponsorship: National Institutes of Health, Division of Research Resources

Program: CAREER MINI-INTERNSHIPS

Description: assist placing volunteers in private veterinary practices.

Additional information: the college is fortunate to participate in the Health Sciences Minority Program, which provides programs at all levels for minority students who wish to enter one of the health professions, including veterinary medicine.

Contact person: Jaki Cottingham-Zierdt, 1-125 M005 Tower, 515 Delaware Street SE, Minneapolis MN 55455; telephone: (612) 624-9400.

Mississippi State University

Program: BOARD OF TRUSTEES OF STATE INSTITUTIONS OF HIGHER LEARNING VETERINARY MEDICINE MINORITY LOAN/SCHOLARSHIP PROGRAM

Description: a financial assistance program for Mississippi residents who are underrepresented minorities. Must be a Mississippi resident and agree to work in Mississippi for at least three years following graduation.

Contact person: Dottie Strain, Director of Student Financial Aid, Mississippi Institutions of Higher Learning, 3825 Ridgewood Road, Jackson, MS 39211-6453; telephone: (601) 982-6570.

University of Missouri

Program: EXPLORATIONS IN VETERINARY MEDICINE

Description: a two-week program to give selected high school junior or senior students an opportunity to observe and assist in veterinary medical research activities and services offered through the Veterinary Medical Diagnostic Laboratory and the Veterinary Medical Teaching Hospital. Travel expenses, room, and board are provided. A stipend is also offered for miscellaneous expenses.

Eligibility: high school junior or senior ethnic minority students.

Program dates: Two weeks in July

Contact person: Associate Dean, College of Veterinary Medicine, University of Missouri, Columbia, MO 65211

Program: GATEWAYS TO VETERINARY MEDICINE

Description: a six-week program to give selected college sophomore, junior, or senior students an opportunity to gain experience with faculty researchers and clinicians in the College of Veterinary Medicine. Travel expenses, room, and board are provided. A stipend is also offered for miscellaneous expenses.

Eligibility: college sophomore, junior, and senior students who are ethnic minorities.

Program dates: mid-June into July.

Contact person: Associate Dean, College of Veterinary Medicine, University of Missouri, Columbia MO 65211

North Carolina State University

Program: MINORITY HIGH SCHOOL APPRENTICE PROGRAM

Description: this eight-week summer program is designed to promote interest in veterinary medicine.

Eligibility: students must be either high school juniors or seniors.

Program dates: 8 weeks from mid-June to mid-August.

Contact person: Marva C. Motley, Director, Student Admissions, North Carolina State University, Raleigh NC 27606.

Sponsorship: National Institutes of Health, Division of Research Resources

Program: CVM Summer Workshop

Description: one-week summer workshop for rising sixth graders, designed to introduce participants to the veterinary profession. Offers hands-on science activities.

Eligibility: disadvantaged youth from North Carolina. Teacher or counselor recommendation is required.

Program dates: June (two workshops currently offered).

Contact person: Rhonda Waters, Director, Recruitment, NCSU-CVM, Raleigh NC 27606.

Sponsorship: foundations and private sponsors.

Ohio State University

Program: Young Scholars Program

Description: this summer program is offered to seventh through eleventh grade students from Ohio. It provides hands-on science activities.

Eligibility: disadvantaged students from Ohio who have been recommended by their faculty as having academic potential.

Program dates: June to August each summer.

Sponsorship: this program is provided for by funds from the State of Ohio and The Ohio State University.

Program: Research Apprenticeship Program

Description: this program is designed to expose gifted minority high school students and high school science teachers to research and animal-related activities through linkage with veterinary college faculty. Though research is the major focus of the program, academic instruction is provided to facilitate scientific knowledge relative to veterinary medicine. A poster presentation of the summer's research project is required at the end of this eight-week program.

Eligibility: eleventh and twelfth grade students from Ohio who have demonstrated academic success and have indicated veterinary medicine as a career choice; high school science teachers who set science education as a high priority.

Program dates: June through August.

Contact person: Robert Suber, Office of Minority Affairs, The Ohio State University, 1800 Cannon Drive, Columbus OH 43210.

Sponsorship: this program is sponsored by a grant from the U.S. Department of Health and Human Services.

Program: Summer Research Opportunity Program

Description: this program is designed to promote the migration of minority undergraduate students into graduate research educational programs by providing them with summer research experiences. The student is provided with his or her individualized research problem by a faculty mentor and expected to carry that research through to publication.

Eligibility: the student must have completed two years of college work and have achieved at least a 2.5 cumulative grade point average. The student must be an underrepresented minority or economically disadvantaged.

Contact person: Jean D. Dickerscheid, Graduate School, The Ohio State University, 230 North Oval Mall, Columbus OH 43210.

Sponsorship: this program is sponsored by the Big Ten Consortium for Institutional Studies.

The University of Tennessee

Program: MINORITY HIGH SCHOOL STUDENT RESEARCH APPRENTICE PROGRAM

Description: high school students are given the opportunity to work in biomedical research laboratories of the College of Veterinary Medicine or in the small and large animal clinics of the Veterinary Teaching Hospital.

Eligibility: high school juniors or seniors.

Program dates: mid-June to mid-August.

Contact person: Dr. Terry Schultz, Minority High School Student Research Apprenticeship Program, College of Veterinary Medicine, The University of Tennessee, P.O. Box 1071, Knoxville TN 37901-1071.

Texas A & M University

Program: VETERINARY RESEARCH APPRENTICE PROGRAM

Description: gives high school students an opportunity to work in a research laboratory.

Eligibility: graduating high school seniors.

Program dates: early June through early August.

Contact person: Mr. Lyndon Kurtz, Associate Director, Biomedical Science, College of Veterinary Medicine, Texas A & M University, College Station TX 77843-4465; telephone: (409) 845-4941.

Program: VETERINARY ENRICHMENT

Description: three-day program for 40 high school students.

Eligibility: college sophomore, junior, and senior minority students.

Program dates: two weeks in early June.

Contact person: Mr. Lyndon Kurtz, Associate Director, Biomedical Science, College of Veterinary Medicine, Texas A & M University, College Station TX 77843-4465; telephone: (409) 845-4941.

Tufts University

Program: MINORITY HIGH SCHOOL APPRENTICE PROGRAM

Description: high school students assist in ongoing research projects at the veterinary school.

Eligibility: high school students interested in science.

Program dates: mid-June to mid-August; application deadline: mid-May.

Contact person: Rebecca Russo, Director of Admissions, School of Veterinary Medicine, Tufts University, 200 Westboro Road, North Grafton MA 01536.

Tuskegee University

Program: HEALTH CAREERS OPPORTUNITY PROGRAM

Description: this 8-week preadmission activity is designed to facilitate the entry of "high risk" students and provide the skills necessary for successful transition to the professional school.

Eligibility: participation is targeted to minority and disadvantaged students who have completed at least two years of college and all preveterinary prerequisites. Participation is restricted to persons who have applied to the Tuskegee University School of Veterinary Medicine and who have been selected by the Veterinary Admissions Committee to attend.

Program dates: summer before matriculation.

Contact person: Associate Dean, School of Veterinary Medicine, Tuskegee AL 36088.

Sponsorship: this program is sponsored by a grant from the U.S. Dept. of Health and Human Services.

Program: VETERINARY SCIENCE TRAINING, EDUCATION AND PREPARATION INSTITUTES FOR MINORITY STUDENTS (VET-STEP I AND II)

Description: Consists of two one-week programs designed to encourage high-achieving minority students to consider veterinary medicine as a career choice. Held in mid-July, the program offers students progressive learning experiences in reading comprehension, note-taking, medical vocabulary, etc. Vet-Step II only accepts students who have participated in Vet-Step I. The program is sponsored by the U.S. Department of Health and Human Services.

Eligibility: Vet-Step I accepts 25 students from grades 10 and 11; Vet-Step II accepts students from grade 12. Minority, high school honor students interested in the biomedical sciences are eligible to apply.

Contact person: Mr. Philip H. Mitchell, Coordinator, Vet-Step Program, School of Veterinary Medicine, Tuskegee University, Tuskegee, AL 36080.

Virginia Polytechnic Institute and State University

The college recognizes the need to ensure that minorities and disadvantaged populations are properly represented in the profession. As a result, the college has established a Committee on Diversity to seek out highly qualified minority and underrepresented students.

A program was implemented to admit a limited number of students who graduate from an honors curriculum at selected institutions. The standards for admission through this program equal or exceed those of the regular admissions process. A limited number of scholarships are available to assist minority students. Those desiring more information about this program are encouraged to contact the admissions office of the college at Blacksburg or College Park.

Washington State University

Program: MINORITY HIGH SCHOOL STUDENT RESEARCH APPRENTICE PROGRAM

Description: an eight-week summer program designed to promote interest in research on the part of ethnic minority high school students. Stipends are provided.

Eligibility: students must be either high school juniors or seniors.

Program dates: 8 weeks from mid-June to mid-August.

Contact person: Ms. Sharon Cross, Department of Veterinary Microbiology and Pathology, Washington State University, Pullman WA 99164-7040.

Sponsorship: The National Center for Research Resources of the National Institutes of Health.

Program: SHORT-TERM RESEARCH PROGRAM FOR ETHNIC MINORITY PREBACCALAUREATE COLLEGE STUDENTS

Description: a three-month summer program designed to promote interest in research by prebaccalaureate ethnic minority students. Focus of the program is a hands-on research project supervised by a faculty member. Stipends are provided.

Eligibility: Ethnic minority prebaccalaureate students majoring in a field of biology.

Program dates: three months during the summer designed to fit the summer vacation dates of the colleges and universities from which the ethnic minority prebaccalaureate students are recruited.

Contact person: Ms. Sharon Cross, Department of Veterinary Microbiology and Pathology, Washington State University, Pullman WA 99164-7040.

Sponsorship: The National Heart, Lung and Blood Institute of the National Institutes of Health.

Program: SHORT-TERM RESEARCH TRAINING PROGRAM FOR VETERINARY STUDENTS

Description: a three-month summer program designed to promote interest in research by veterinary students. Emphasis is on a hands-on research project supervised by a faculty member with a research program. Stipends are provided.

Eligibility: Washington-Oregon-Idaho program veterinary students or ethnic minority veterinary students from other North American colleges of veterinary medicine.

Program dates: three months in the summer dependent upon the summer vacation of the College of Veterinary Medicine in which the veterinary student is enrolled.

Contact person: Ms. Sharon Cross, Department of Veterinary Microbiology and Pathology, Washington State University, Pullman WA 99164-7040.

Sponsorship: The National Center for Research Resources and the National Heart, Lung, and Blood Institute of the National Institutes of Health.

University of Wisconsin

Program: MINORITY HIGH SCHOOL RESEARCH APPRENTICE PROGRAM

Description: high school students are given the opportunity to work in research laboratories at the college.

Eligibility: high school juniors and seniors.

Program dates: mid-June to August.

Contact person: Susan Hyland, Associate Dean, School of Veterinary Medicine, University of Wisconsin-Madison, 2015 Linden Drive West, Madison WI 53706.

Senior veterinary students from Ohio State were photographed while serving their rotation in zoo animal medicine at the Columbus Zoo elephant house.

PHOTO BY JOHN JEWETT

FINANCIAL AID INFORMATION

Financing your veterinary medical education requires careful planning, good money management skills, and a willingness to make short-term sacrifices to achieve long-range goals.

Many of you may have already received some type of financial assistance during your undergraduate education. If so, you are probably already somewhat familiar with the process, and know that the rules and regulations governing programs can and do change periodically.

As a professional student, you will be entering a partnership with the financial aid office, which will require you to complete the appropriate financial aid forms accurately, meet required deadlines, and submit any additional information that may be requested. In return, the financial aid office will determine your aid eligibility and make awards based on the available programs. Your financial aid eligibility takes into account the cost of your education minus any other available resources. Amounts of assistance and the school policies for awarding assistance vary from one veterinary medical school to another and from year to year.

Any questions or concerns that you may have about this topic need to be directed to each of the appropriate financial aid offices to ensure that you receive accurate information and guidance.

VETERINARY MEDICAL ORGANIZATIONS

AVMA   American Veterinary Medical Association
                1931 North Meacham Road, Suite 100
                Schaumburg IL 60173-4360
                (800) 248-2862

AAVMC   Association of American Veterinary Medical Colleges
                1101 Vermont Avenue NW, Suite 710
                Washington DC 20005-3521
                (202) 371-9195

Information About Standardized Tests

Most veterinary medical colleges require one or more standardized tests: the *Medical College Admission Test* (MCAT), *Veterinary College Admission Test* (VCAT), or *Graduate Record Examinations* (GRE). For an examination application and information on test dates, contact the testing agencies listed below:

GRE
             Graduate Record Examinations
             P.O. Box 6000
             Princeton NJ 08541-6000
             (609) 771-7670 (Princeton, N.J.)
             also: (510) 654-1200 (Oakland, Calif.)

MCAT
             Medical College Admission Test
             MCAT Program Office
             P.O. Box 4056
             Iowa City IA 52243
             (319) 337-1357

VCAT
             The Psychological Corporation
             Veterinary College Admission Test
             555 Academic Court
             San Antonio TX 78204
             (210) 921-8794
             (800) 622-3231

AUBURN UNIVERSITY   ALABAMA

Committee on Admissions
College of Veterinary Medicine
217 Goodwin Center
Auburn University AL 36849
Telephone: (334) 844-2685

The College of Veterinary Medicine at Auburn University is located in south central Alabama on Interstate 85 between Montgomery and Atlanta. The university is known for its friendly small-campus atmosphere, despite having more than 21,000 students. In 1990 the town was listed among the top fifty U.S. cities with fewer than 50,000 people.

Veterinary medicine began as a department at Auburn in 1892 and became a college in 1907. Today it is situated in modern facilities on 240 acres one mile from the main Auburn campus. In addition, the college has a 700-acre research farm five miles from its campus. The college is fully accredited by the American Veterinary Medical Association.

Application Information

Applications available: August 1

Application deadline: November 1

Application fee: $35.00; applicants who have not previously attended Auburn University are also required to submit a university processing fee of $25.00.

Residency implications: priority is given to Alabama residents based on length of residency. Auburn contracts with Kentucky for 34 positions.

Auburn has a quota for the admission of nonresidents (10). All nonresidents must apply through the Veterinary Medical Colleges Application Service (VMCAS). VMCAS applications are available August 1. Individuals must be citizens of the U.S., but they may come from any state; they must have a 3.0 grade point average (GPA) on a scale where 4.0 is an *A* and must meet all other academic requirements.

 (Veterinary Medical Colleges Application Service (VMCAS)): required for all nonresidents.

Prerequisites for Admission

The following subjects may be waived if the individual has a baccalaureate degree: freshman English; world history, world literature, or technology and civilization.

38

Electives must be earned in the humanities and fine arts and the social sciences to meet the liberal education requirements of the university. These may be waived for individuals with baccalaureate degrees. Science electives must be 300 level courses.

Three semester-hour courses are accepted as the equivalent in subject matter content of five quarter-hour courses. All transfer courses must be equivalent in hours and content.

Course Requirements and Quarter Hours

English composition	10
Great Books I, II	10
Precalculus with trigonometry	5
Ethics or logic	5
World history, human odyssey, or technology and civilization	9
Social science electives	9
Fine arts elective	3
Fundamentals of chemistry with laboratory	15
Organic chemistry with laboratory	10
Introductory physics	15
Principles of biology with laboratory	5
Animal biology with laboratory	5
Animal biochemistry and nutrition	5
Science electives	8
Total quarter-hour credits:	114

Required undergraduate GPA: a minimum grade point average of **at least** 2.5 on a 4.0 scale is required, with the minimum acceptable grade for required courses being *C*-minus. Applicants who do not classify as Alabama residents must have a 3.0 GPA on a 4-point scale, except for Kentucky applicants under SREB contract. The mean grade point average of the most recent entering class was 3.35.

Course completion deadline: prerequisite courses must be completed by June 15 prior to matriculation.

Standardized examinations: Graduate Record Examination, General Aptitude subtest, is required. The GRE may be taken no later than October in the year of application.

Additional Requirements and Considerations

Animal/veterinary experience
Recommendations/evaluations, both personal and regarding animal experience
Extracurricular and community service activities
Employment record
Narrative statement of purpose
Neatness of application
Major science courses must have been completed within the previous six calendar years

Summary of Admission Procedure

Auburn University has a three-part admission procedure, which entails an objective evaluation of academic credentials, a subjective review of personal credentials, and a personal interview.

Timetable

Application deadline: November 1
Notification of interview: January
Date interviews are held: March–April
Date acceptances mailed: approximately April 10
Applicant's response date: April 15

Deposit (to hold place in class): none required

Deferments: not considered

Expenses for the 1995–96 Academic Year

Tuition and fees

Resident	$3,168.00
Nonresident	
Contract student	$3,168.00
Contract nonresident	$7,128.00

Living expenses (estimated) $6,000.00

1994–95 Admissions Summary

	Number of Applicants	Number of New Entrants
In-state	145	48
Contract	82	34
Out-of-state	195	10
Total:	422	92

School begins: September 21, 1995

UNIVERSITY OF CALIFORNIA

CALIFORNIA

Office of the Dean-Student Programs
School of Veterinary Medicine
University of California
Davis, CA 95616
Telephone: (916) 752-1383

The University of California, Davis (UCD) campus is adjacent to the city of Davis, which is fourteen miles west of Sacramento, the state capital, and seventy-two miles northeast of San Francisco. Davis is known as the "city of bicycles." The community is closely tied to the university yet has developed its own recreational, cultural, and community outlets. Winter temperatures are generally mild and rarely fall below freezing. Summers are sunny, hot, and dry. Weather in the spring and fall is the most pleasant in the state. UCD is an outstanding research and training institution with approximately 23,000 undergraduate, graduate, and professional students enrolled in three colleges and professional schools (Veterinary Medicine, Medicine, Law, and Management). The modern educational buildings and research facilities are situated on over 5200 acres at Davis and ten off-campus field stations. UCD is the home of the Veterinary Medical Teaching Hospital, the California Primate Center, the California Diagnostic Laboratory, and the Institute for Toxicology and Environmental Health. There are many innovative programs at UCD with many international students. The school is fully committed to recruiting students with diverse racial backgrounds.

Application Information

Applications available: July 15

Application deadline: November 1

Application fee: See VMCAS

Residency implications: priority is given to California residents. California accepts no more than two applicants from WICHE states (Alaska, Arizona, Hawaii, Montana, Nevada, New Mexico, North Dakota, Utah, and Wyoming), and California may accept a small number of uniquely qualified nonresident applicants.

(Veterinary Medical Colleges Application Service (VMCAS)): required for all residents and nonresidents.

Prerequisites for Admission

The following represent the basic requirements for admission:

Course Requirements and Quarter Hours

General chemistry	10
Organic chemistry	4
Biochemistry	2

41

Physics	4
Biology	7
Systemic physiology	4
Vertebrate embryology	3
Genetics	3
English composition	3
Additional English	6
Humanities and social sciences	8
Statistics	3
Total quarter-hour credits:	57

Required undergraduate GPA: a minimum grade point average of 2.5 on a 4-point scale is required. Applicants accepted into the Class of 1999 had a mean cumulative GPA of 3.4.

Course completion deadline: all prerequisite courses must be completed by the time a student plans to enroll.

Standardized examinations: Graduate Record Examination (aptitude section and subject test in biology) is required. The latest acceptable test date for applicants to the Class of 2000 is October 1995. Date of oldest acceptable scores is October 1990.

Average GRE scores for the class admitted in 1995 are verbal 599, quantitative 679, analytical 700, and advanced biology 735.

Additional Requirements and Considerations

Veterinary/animal experience
Letters of evaluation (three)
Narrative statement of motivation/career goals
Accuracy and neatness of application
Interview

Summary of Admission Procedure

Timetable

Application deadline: November 1
Notification of interview: early February
Date interviews are held: end of February to mid-March
Date acceptances mailed: by April 1
Applicant's response date: April 15

Deposit (to hold place in class): none required

Deferments: not considered

Expenses for the 1995–96 Academic Year

Tuition and fees

Resident	$ 7,780.00
Nonresident	$15,479.00
Contract student	$ 7,780.00

Living expenses (estimated) $10,500.00
    (includes books, supplies, transportation, and personal
    expenses)

1994–95 Admissions Summary

	Number of Applicants	*Number of New Entrants*
In-state	438	99
Contract	22	2
Out-of-state	92	7
Total:	552	108

School begins: Early September

Evaluation Criteria

	% weight
Grades	30
Test scores	30
Interview	20
References	6
Essay	14

Special Academic Programs for Veterinary Students

In order to recruit, train, and graduate veterinarians with preparation in specific areas of the field of veterinary medicine, the School of Veterinary Medicine has initiated five programs combining the D.V.M. with B.S., M.S., or Ph.D. degrees. These programs emphasize: 1) *Avian Medicine/Science,* in conjunction with the Avian Sciences Department on the Davis Campus; 2) *Food Animal Production,* in conjunction with the Animal Science Department on the Davis Campus; 3) *Food Safety,* in conjunction with the Food Science and Technology Department on the Davis Campus; 4) *Wildlife Health,* in conjunction with the Department of Wildlife and Fisheries Biology on the Davis Campus; and 5) *Academic Graduate Education,* in conjunction with the UCD graduate group of the student's choice. Combined Ph.D. degree arrangements are made after admission to the D.V.M. program. Applicants who already have B.S., M.S., or Ph.D. may wish to emphasize one of these areas during their studies, with the goal of entering the specific area as a career choice after receiving the D.V.M.

COLORADO STATE UNIVERSITY

Office of the Dean
College of Veterinary Medicine and Biomedical Sciences
Colorado State University
Fort Collins CO 80523
Telephone: (970) 491-7051

Colorado State University is located in Fort Collins, a small city of about 100,000 in the eastern foothills of the Rocky Mountains about sixty miles north of Denver. Fort Collins has a pleasant climate and offers many cultural and recreational activities. Many of the state's ski areas lie within a short driving distance, making some of the best skiing in the world accessible. The nearby river canyons and mountain parks are beautiful scenic attractions and provide opportunities for hiking, fishing, photography, camping, and biking.

The College of Veterinary Medicine and Biomedical Sciences is composed of five major buildings that house the departments of anatomy and neurobiology, microbiology, environmental health, pathology, physiology, and radiological health sciences. The Veterinary Teaching Hospital, one of the world's largest and best-equipped, houses the clinical sciences department. The hospital attracts a large caseload and offers students a wide variety of clinical experiences.

Application Information

Applications available: August 1

Application deadline: November 1

Application fee: $40.00

Residency implications: Approximately half of each class is made up of Colorado residents.

Approximately half of places contracted through WICHE [must be certified by WICHE] and are allocated as follows: Alaska 1, Arizona 14, Utah 7, Hawaii 3, Montana 6, New Mexico 16, North Dakota 2, Wyoming 6, and Nevada 2.

Each WICHE state reimburses Colorado for educational costs, and the WICHE students pay in-state tuition and fees.

Colorado accepts a limited number of applicants from states other than Colorado or WICHE contract states. Such applicants must agree to be accountable for the full cost of their professional education, as defined by Colorado statute.

(Veterinary Medical Colleges Application Service (VMCAS)): no participation.

Prerequisites for Admission

Course Requirements and Semester Credit Hours

Laboratory associated with a biology course	1
Genetics	3
Laboratory associated with a chemistry course	1
Biochemistry	3
Physics with laboratory	4
Statistics/biostatistics	3
English composition	3
Social sciences and humanities	12
Electives	38
Total:	68

Required undergraduate GPA: there is no "required" GPA. The mean GPA for the class admitted in 1995 was 3.00 on a 4-point scale.

Course completion deadline: transcripts with final grades, including all required courses, must be received by July 15 prior to matriculation.

Standardized examinations: Graduate Record Examination is required; must be taken within the last five years prior to application. The latest acceptable test date is the one in October of the year prior to matriculation. Mean GRE scores for the class admitted in 1995 were verbal 543, quantitative 611, analytical 631.

Additional Requirements and Considerations

Animal/veterinary experience
Recommendations/evaluations, preferably from the following:
  Academic (one from either recent academic advisor or college professor)
  Employer (one from any employer)
  Veterinarian
Essay
Extracurricular and/or community service activities
Quality of academic program (course load, challenging curriculum, honors)
Ethnic minority/disadvantaged background

Summary of Admission Procedure

Timetable

Application deadline: November 1
Notification of interview: February 20
Date interviews are held: March 1–7
Date acceptances mailed: April 1

Deposit (to hold place in class): none required

Deferments: not considered

Expenses for the 1995–96 Academic Year

Each WICHE state reimburses Colorado for educational costs and the WICHE students pay resident tuition and fees.

Tuition and fees (first-year students only)
Resident $ 8,140.00
Nonresident
    Contract student $ 8,140.00
    Other nonresident $27,440.00

1993–94 Admissions Summary

	Number of Applicants	Number of New Entrants
In-state	296	61
Contract (WICHE)	228	51
"At large"	240	20
Total:	764	132

School begins: August 21, 1995

Evaluation Criteria	*% weight*	*points*
Grades	37	700
Test scores	11	200
Animal/veterinary experience, quality of academic program, essay, activities and achievements, references	26	500
Minority status	5	100
Disadvantage	5	100
Interview*	16	300

* Not all applicants receive an interview

Special Admissions Programs

Early Admission Program: may request consideration if GPA is 3.80 or better with 68 credits completed and GRE is at least 1750 (total of scores for verbal, quantitative, and analytical subtests).

Vet Start: guaranteed admission for a limited number of qualified minority and/ or disadvantaged high school students attending the Colorado State University preveterinary program. Students must be Colorado residents or be eligible for future WICHE certification. Separate application procedure.

CORNELL UNIVERSITY   NEW YORK

Office of Admissions
College of Veterinary Medicine at Cornell
S1 006 Schurman Hall
Cornell University
Ithaca, NY 14853-6401
Telephone: (607) 253-3700

Cornell is located in Ithaca, a city of about 30,000 in the Finger Lakes region of New York State, a beautiful area of rolling hills, deep valleys, scenic gorges, and clear lakes. The University's 740-acre campus is bounded on two sides by gorges and waterfalls. Open countryside, state parks, and year-round opportunities for outdoor recreation, including excellent sailing, swimming, skiing, hiking, and other activities, are only minutes away.

Ithaca is one hour by air and a five-hour drive from New York City, and other major metropolitan areas are easily accessible. Direct commercial flights connect Ithaca with New York, Boston, Chicago, Pittsburgh, Washington, and other cities.

The tradition of academic excellence, the cultural vigor of a distinguished university, and the magnificent setting create a stimulating environment for graduate study. The college opened a new Veterinary Education Center in 1993 and extensive new clinical and research facilities in 1995.

Application Information

Applications available: July

Application deadline: October 1

Application fee: $60.00 for direct applications (not through VMCAS). There is a supplemental application and fee for VMCAS applicants.

Residency implications: 60 places reserved for New York State residents. The College of Veterinary Medicine at Cornell currently has contracts with New Hampshire, New Jersey, and Puerto Rico. There are a variable number of places available for nonresidents.

(Veterinary Medical Colleges Application Service (VMCAS)): optional for all nonresidents.

The College of Veterinary Medicine at Cornell currently has contracts with New Hampshire, New Jersey, and Puerto Rico. There are a variable number of places available for nonresidents.

Prerequisites for Admission

Course Requirements and Minimum Semester Hours

English composition*	6
Biology or zoology, full year with laboratory	6
Physics, full year with laboratory	6
Inorganic (general) chemistry, full year with laboratory	6
Organic chemistry, full year with laboratory	6
Biochemistry**	4
General microbiology, with laboratory	3
Electives	53
Total Semester-Hour Credits:	90

* Three credits may be satisfied by a course in public speaking.
** This should be a complete upper division course in general biochemistry; half of a two-semester sequence will not meet this requirement.

Required undergraduate GPA: Cornell does not have a GPA requirement, but the grade range of those admitted tends to be 3.0–4.0. The mean GPA for the Class of 1999 was 3.57.

Course completion deadline: all but seven credits of the prerequisite course work should be completed at the time of application, with at least one semester of any two-semester series completed. Any outstanding prerequisites must be completed by the end of the spring term prior to matriculation.

Standardized examinations: Graduate Record Examination (verbal and quantitative subtests) is required. The latest acceptable test date for applicants to the Class of 2000 is the October 1995 exam. The Class of 1999 had a mean score of 1307 (verbal 628 and quantitative 683). Test scores older than five years are not acceptable.

Additional Requirements and Considerations

Animal/veterinary experience, knowledge, and motivation
Recommendations/evaluations
    Academic advisor
    Animal experience employers
    Nonveterinary work–related experiences
Essay
Extracurricular and/or community service activities
Demonstrated leadership skills
Quality of academic program

SUMMARY OF ADMISSION PROCEDURE

The admission procedure at the College of Veterinary Medicine at Cornell consists of two phases: an objective evaluation of academic credentials and a subjective review of overall application.

Timetable

Application deadline: October 1
Offers of admission sent: early March

Information sessions at the college: mid-March to early April
Applicant's response date: April 15; applicants (alternates) accepted after the
initial response date will have two weeks to respond to an offer of admission
from the college.

Deposit (to hold place in class): $500.00

Deferments: considered on an individual basis, but ordinarily granted only for
illness or other problem beyond the voluntary control of the applicant.

Expenses for the 1995–96 Academic Year

Proposed tuition and fees (not finally approved at time of submission)
Resident	$12,650.00
Nonresident	
Contract student	$12,650.00
Other nonresident	$17,000.00
Books and supplies	$ 725.00

Living expenses (estimated)
Room and board	$ 6,150.00
Personal	$ 3,400.00

1994–95 Admissions Summary

	Number of Applicants	Number of New Entrants
In-state	255	63
Contract	55	4
Out-of-state	299	15
Total:	609	82

School begins: August 31, 1995; orientation, August 29–30

Evaluation Criteria

	% weight
Grades	30
Test scores (GRE)	30
Animal/veterinary experience	20
References, essay, quality of academic program, and nonacademic activities	20

Special Admissions Programs

Guaranteed Admissions Program: highly qualified students may apply in spring
of their sophomore year for early admission to the D.V.M. professional program.
Their outstanding academic qualifications can guarantee them admission at the
completion of their junior year or, if they choose, after graduation with a baccalaureate degree. With their professional education assured, they are free to plan
an undergraduate curriculum that broadens their general education or focuses
on a specialized interest.

The application and prerequisite requirements are the same as for other applicants, except that they must have no grade less than B in any required course.
Students who have not satisfied all of the prerequisite coursework must complete

49

it by the end of spring term prior to matriculation in the professional curriculum. The latest acceptable GRE score test date for guaranteed admission is the February test. The evaluation process is the same as for other applicants, except that completed applications must be sent to the Admissions Office with a postmark no later than April 1.

Special Programs for Veterinary Students

Leadership Training Program: this program targets gifted students who are potential leaders in the profession. Major objectives of the program are to acquaint the participating students with career opportunities for veterinarians in academic institutions, government, and industry, to assist them in planning their careers, and to establish a professional network that will encourage future interaction among the program participants.

Successful candidates will be awarded fellowships that will enable them to spend 10 weeks in the summer at Cornell. Student fellows will engage in faculty-directed research. They also will take part in professional enrichment activities which have been selected for their excellence and relevance to the program. Features of the program include $3,000 honorarium, free in-residence housing, research experience, attendance at seminars and conferences, and career counseling. After completion of at least one year in an accredited D.V.M. program, veterinary students are eligible to apply. For information or to apply, contact: Graduate Education Coordinator, S1 006 Schurman Hall, Cornell University.

UNIVERSITY OF FLORIDA

College of Veterinary Medicine
Admissions Office
P.O. Box 100125
University of Florida
Gainesville FL 32610-0125
Telephone: (904) 392-4700, ext. 5300

The University of Florida is located in Gainesville, a college town of 120,000 in north central Florida midway between the Gulf of Mexico and the Atlantic Ocean. Changes in season are marked, but winters are mild and permit year-round participation in outdoor activities.

The university accommodates about 34,000 students with programs in almost all disciplines. The College of Veterinary Medicine is a component of the Institute of Food and Agriculture Sciences (which also includes Agriculture and Forest Resources and Conservation). It is also one of six colleges affiliated with the Health Science Center (the other five are Dentistry, Health-Related Professions, Medicine, Nursing, and Pharmacy).

The veterinary curriculum is an eight-semester program consisting of core curriculum and elective experiences. The core provides the body of knowledge and skills common to all veterinarians. The first four semesters concentrate primarily on basic medical sciences. Students are additionally introduced to physical diagnosis, radiology, and clinical problems during the first year. The core also includes experience in each of the clinical areas. Elective areas of concentration permit students to investigate further the aspects of both basic and clinical sciences most relevant to their interests.

Application Information

Applications available: July 1

Application deadline: November 1

Application fee: See VMCAS

Residency implications: priority is given to Florida residents, and Florida has no contractual agreements. Nonresidents are considered in very limited numbers (not more than 10% of any entering class).

(Veterinary Medical Colleges Application Service (VMCAS)): required for all residents and nonresidents.

Prerequisites for Admission

Course Requirements and Semester Hours

Biology (general, genetics, microbiology)	15
Chemistry (inorganic, organic, biochemistry)	19
Physics	7
Mathematics (calculus, statistics)	6
Animal Science	
(introduction to animal science, animal nutrition)	8
Humanities	9
Social sciences	6
English (two courses in English composition)	6
Electives	at least 4
Total Semester-Hour Credits:	80

Required undergraduate GPA: a minimum GPA of 2.75 on a 4-point scale. The Class of 1998 had an overall mean science prerequisite GPA of 3.15.

Course completion deadline: prerequisite courses must be completed by the end of the spring term prior to admission.

Standardized examinations: Graduate Record Examination is required. October 1995 is the latest acceptable test date for applicants to the Class of 2000. Mean scores for the Class of 1999 were verbal 548, quantitative 628. Year of oldest acceptable scores is 1986.

Additional Requirements and Considerations

Animal/veterinary experience
Recommendations/evaluations
  Personal
  Animal work experience
  Academic advisor
Honors and awards received
Extracurricular activities
Essay

Summary of Admission Procedure

The admission procedure of the University of Florida consists of three parts: each applicant's file is reviewed; selected applicants are each interviewed for about twenty minutes by three faculty members; final selection of new class takes place.

Timetable

Application deadline: November 1
Notification of interview: February 15
Date interviews are held: during March
Date acceptances mailed: April 1
Applicant's response date: May 1

Deposit (to hold a place in class): none required

Deferments: considered on an individual basis

Expenses for the 1995–96 Academic Year

Tuition and fees

Resident	$ 6,612.00
Nonresident	
Contract student	N/A
Other nonresident	$16,820.00

Living expenses (estimated)	$ 9,482.00

1993–94 Admissions Summary

	Number of Applicants	Number of New Entrants
In-state	205	67
Contract	N/A	N/A
Out-of-state	282	13
Total:	487	80

School begins: August 21, 1995; freshman orientation on August 17–18.

THE UNIVERSITY OF GEORGIA   GEORGIA

College of Veterinary Medicine
The University of Georgia
Athens GA 30602-7372
Telephone: (706) 542-5728

The University of Georgia is located in Athens-Clarke County, with a population of 86,000. Georgia's "Classic City" is a prospering community that reflects the charm of the Old South while growing in culture and industry. Athens is just over an hour away from the north Georgia mountains and the metropolitan area of Atlanta, and just over five hours away from the Atlantic coast.

In 1785, Georgia became the first state to grant a charter for a state-supported university. In 1801 the first students came to the newly formed frontier town of Athens. The University of Georgia has grown into an institution with thirteen schools and colleges and more than 2,700 faculty members and 29,000 students.

Application Information

Applications available: August 1

Application deadline: November 1

Application fee: $30.00

Residency implications: Georgia residents may compete for up to 54 available spaces. Georgia retains 23 positions for contract students. Contracts include South Carolina (maximum 17) and West Virginia (maximum six). In addition, up to ten "at large" applicants may be admitted as part of the contract program.

(Veterinary Medical Colleges Application Service (VMCAS)): required for all nonresidents.

Prerequisites for Admission

Course Requirements and Quarter Hours

English	9
Humanities and social studies	20
General biology	10
Advanced biological science	10
Chemistry	
Inorganic	10
Organic	10
Physics	15
Biochemistry	5
Total Quarter-Hour Credits:	89

Required undergraduate GPA: a minimum of 2.70 on a 4-point scale. The mean GPA of the Class of 1999 was 3.45.

Course completion deadline: prerequisite courses must be completed by the end of the spring term preceding entry.

Standardized Examinations: applicants must complete the general tests of the *Graduate Record Examination* (GRE) and *Veterinary College Admission Test* (VCAT) within the three years immediately preceding the deadline for receipt of applications (November 1). All standardized tests should be completed by December 15 and the results officially reported to the college Office of Academic Affairs by February 1 of the following year. GRE and VCAT scores should be sent directly to the College of Veterinary Medicine, University of Georgia, Athens, GA., 30602-7372.

For the Class of 1999, the mean scores for the verbal and quantitative portions of the GRE were verbal 587, quantitative 666; for this entering class the average VCAT score was 83.

Additional Requirements and Considerations

Animal experience
Background for veterinary medicine
Recommendations/evaluations
   Academic advisors
   Animal experience employers
   Major professional and department head (graduate students)
Essay

Summary of Admission Procedure

The University of Georgia admission procedure includes a file evaluation. There are no interviews, but applicants are invited to a College orientation.

Timetable

Application deadline: November 1
Date acceptances mailed: March or April
Applicant's response date: April 15

Deposit (to hold place in class): $100.00; $500.00 for "at large" students.

Deferments: are considered to complete a degree, for health problems, or because of financial problems.

Expenses for the 1995–96 Academic Year

Tuition and fees (approximate)	
Resident	$ 3,250.00
Nonresident	
Contract student	$ 3,250.00
Contract fee ("at large" students)	$10,150.00
Other nonresident	N/A
Living expenses (estimated)	$8,000–$9,000

GEORGIA

1995 Admissions Summary

	Number of Applicants	Number Accepted
In-state	184	54
Contract (SREB)	57	23
"At large"	185	10
Total:	426	87

School begins: August 21, 1995.

Evaluation Criteria

	% weight
Grades	29
Test scores	57
Animal/veterinary experience, essay references (combined file evaluation)	14

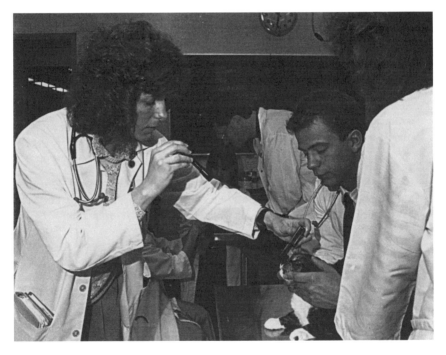

Students and a clinical instructor who specializes in cats are performing an examination on the cat's retina at the small animal hospital at The Ohio State University College of Veterinary Medicine.

PHOTO BY JOHN J. SWARTZ

University of Illinois

Office of Admissions and Records
College of Veterinary Medicine
University of Illinois at Urbana-Champaign
Administration Building
506 South Wright Street
Urbana IL 61801
Telephone: (217) 333-1192

The University of Illinois is in Urbana-Champaign, a community of about 100,000 people located 140 miles south of Chicago. It is served by four airlines, three interstate highways, bus, and rail. The twin cities and university make a pleasant community with easy access to all areas and facilities. The university has about 35,000 students and more than 11,000 faculty and staff members. It is known for its high-quality academic programs and its exceptional resources and facilities. The university library has the largest collection of any public university and ranks third among all U.S. academic libraries. The university also has outstanding cultural and sports facilities and activities.

The College of Veterinary Medicine is located at the south edge of the campus in a large physical plant built in phases since 1971. In addition to approximately 340 students, the college has about 100 graduate students plus a full complement of residents and interns. There are more than 100 full-time faculty with research interests in a variety of biomedical sciences and clinical areas. This research activity allows a variety of interactions and employment for students. The college also offers students a stimulating core-elective curriculum to prepare for a career in almost any area of the profession.

Application Information

Applications available: October 15

Application deadline: November 1, nonresident early decision deadline; November 1, regular cycle admissions.

Application fee: $30.00

Residency implications: priority is given to Illinois residents; Illinois has no contractual agreements. Illinois offers positions to 20–30 nonresidents with superior qualifications. All nonresidents are given equal consideration.

(Veterinary Medical Colleges Application Service (VMCAS)): optional for all nonresidents.

Prerequisites for Admission

The academic requirements for application to the College of Veterinary Medicine can be met through one of two pathways: Plan A or Plan B. Those considering a career in veterinary medicine should have a good foundation in biological sciences and chemistry, including biochemistry, and should consider the specific courses listed in Plan A as a minimum knowledge base for success in the curriculum. In addition, a course or courses concerning livestock production and animal ethology are highly desirable for all students. Those seeking a career in veterinary medicine related to agriculture should consider additional background in nutrition, livestock management, and the economics of production by working toward a degree in animal science prior to admission to veterinary school.

Plan A

I. B.S. or B.A. degree in any major field of study from an accredited college or university including the following courses (equivalent in content to those required for students majoring in biological sciences):
   a. Eight semester hours of biological sciences with laboratories.
   b. Sixteen semester hours of chemical sciences including organic and biochemistry with laboratories in inorganic and organic chemistry.
   c. Eight semester hours of physics with laboratories.

Plan B

II. Those applying without a bachelor's degree are required to present at least sixty semester hours from an accredited college or university, including forty hours of science courses. The minimum course requirements under Plan B are:
   a. Eight semester hours of biological sciences with laboratories.
   b. Sixteen semester hours of chemical sciences including organic and biochemistry with laboratories in inorganic and organic chemistry.
   c. Eight semester hours of physics with laboratories.
   d. Three semester hours of English composition and an additional three hours of English composition and/or speech.
   e. Twelve semester hours of humanities and social sciences.
   f. Ten semester hours of junior/senior-level courses in addition to the requirements listed above.

Required undergraduate GPA: a cumulative GPA of 3.75 and a minimum science GPA of 3.75 on a 5-point scale are required. The mean GPA for students admitted in 1994 was 4.45 (on a 5.0 scale).

Standardized examinations: Veterinary College of Admission Test (VCAT) is required. The class admitted in 1994 had an average of 77 on the VCAT.

Additional Requirements and Considerations

Animal veterinary knowledge, motivation, and experience
Recommendations/evaluations
   Animal and veterinary experience employer
   Academic advisor
Evidence of leadership, initiative, and responsibility

Summary of Admission Procedure

A two-part admission procedure is used by the University of Illinois. A file evaluation, stressing academic achievement and personal qualities, is followed by a personal interview.

Timetable

Application deadline: November 1; early decision applications from nonresidents are due October 15
No routine interviews
Informational Open House: March; December and January for early decision applicants
Date acceptances mailed: approximately March 1
Applicant's response date: April 15

Deposit (to hold place in class): none required

Deferments: none.

Expenses for the 1995–96 Academic Year

Tuition and fees

Resident	$ 7,098.00
Nonresident	
Contract student	N/A
Other nonresident	$18,678.00

Living Expenses (estimated) $ 7,842.00

1994–95 Admissions Summary

	Number of Applicants	Number of New Entrants
In-state	222	82
Contract	N/A	N/A
Out-of-state	140	5
Total:	362	87

School begins: August 25, 1995

Evaluation Criteria

	% weight
Academic points:	70
cumulative GPA, science GPA, and VCAT test scores are used in a regression equation to calculate academic points.	
Subjective points:	30
veterinary experience, animal experience, evidence of leadership ability, and letters of evaluation.	

Special Programs

The University of Illinois College of Veterinary Medicine offers a core/elective curriculum with enough elective time for students to develop an area of emphasis in a chosen area of the profession. The college is also a member of the Food Animal Production Medicine Consortium, which offers students clinical experiences at any of the six cooperating institutions.

IOWA STATE UNIVERSITY

IOWA

Office of Admissions
Room 100 Alumni Hall
Iowa State University
Ames IA 50011
Telephone: (515) 294-5836
Toll free outside Iowa: 1-(800) 247-3965

The Iowa State University College of Veterinary Medicine is located in the heart of one of the world's most intensive livestock-producing areas, which provides diverse food animal clinical and diagnostic cases. A nearby metropolitan area and a regionally recognized referral veterinary hospital provide experience in companion animal medicine and surgery. A racetrack is located near the college and provides an increasing number of challenging equine patients.

A strong basic science education during the first two years prepares veterinary students for a wide range of clinical experiences during their last two years. The College of Veterinary Medicine provides education in a wide variety of animal species and disciplines and allows fourth-year students to spend time with private practitioners, other colleges, research facilities, and in other educational experiences. Opportunities for research exist in the outstanding research programs in neurobiology, immunobiology, infectious diseases, and numerous other areas, and the National Animal Disease Center and the National Veterinary Services Laboratories located nearby provide additional opportunities. The world's premier State Diagnostic Laboratory is part of the college and provides students with experience that is unmatched by any other veterinary college in the world. Graduates are highly sought after and can typically choose among five or six job offers. A career development and placement service is also helpful.

Application Information

Applications available: July 1 (Iowa State University Office of Admissions)

Application deadline: November 1 (See also "Early Decision Option" under Special Programs below.)

Application fee: $20.00

Residence implications: priority is given to Iowa residents for approximately 60 positions. Iowa contracts on a year-to-year basis with North Dakota and South Dakota for 14 positions. Iowa accepts approximately 25 residents of other states and will consider international students.

Direct application: request application packet from Iowa State University Office of Admissions and submit required information no later than stated deadlines.

60

(Veterinary Medical Colleges Application Service (VMCAS)): optional for non-residents.

Prerequisites for Admission

Course Requirements and Semester Hours

English composition	6
General chemistry, with laboratory	8
Organic chemistry, with laboratory	4
Physics	8
Biology	8
Genetics	3
Arts, humanities, or social sciences	9
Electives	<u>14</u>
Total Semester-Hour Credits:	60

Required undergraduate GPA: the minimum GPA required by Iowa State University is 2.5 on a 4-point scale. The most recent entering class had a mean GPA of 3.41 with a range of 2.82 to 4.00.

Course completion deadline: prerequisite courses must be completed by June 15 prior to matriculation.

Standardized examinations: GRE General Test.

Additional Requirements and Considerations

Recommendations or evaluations from three people not related to the applicant by birth or marriage. College advisors and employers are suggested.

Summary of Admission Procedure

Personal interviews are not conducted at Iowa State. The admission procedure consists of a review of each candidate's application and qualifications:

1. Academic factors (objective)	80%
2. Non-academic and academic factors (subjective)	20%

Timetable

Application deadline: November 1
Interviews: none
Date acceptances mailed: March 1
Applicant's response date: April 15

Deposit (to hold place in class): $150.00

Expenses for the 1995–96 Academic Year

Tuition and fees (subject to change)

Resident	$ 5,444.00
Nonresident	
Contract student	$ 5,444.00
Other nonresident	$14,842.00
Living expenses (estimated)	$10,478.00

1994–95 Admissions Summary

	Number of Applicants	Number of New Entrants
In-state	104	59
Contract	40	25
Out-of-state	546	26
Total:	690	110

School begins: fourth week in August

Evaluation Criteria

	% weight
Grades	50
Test scores (GRE General)	20
Degrees	10
Committee evaluation	20

Special Admissions Programs

Early Decision Option (EDO): The College of Veterinary Medicine will admit a limited number of students for fall 1996 on or before December 1, 1995, according to the procedure stated below. Only a few highly qualified applicants who have completed most of the requirements at the time of application will be admitted under this option.

1. Completed applications and transcripts must be postmarked by October 1, 1995. Late or missing items will automatically disqualify the application for early decision consideration. Failure of transcripts to be postmarked by October 1 is the most common reason for EDO applications to be disqualified. It may take three or more weeks for transcripts to arrive after an applicant has requested they be sent. It is the applicant's responsibility to determine that all requirements have been met and all items have been received.
2. All applicants who meet the EDO deadline will be notified on or before December 1, 1995.
3. Qualified applicants not admitted or considered under EDO will automatically be considered during the regular admission cycle.
4. EDO applicants are not required to submit GRE General Test scores by October 1, but they must submit those scores by February 1, 1996, as must all other applicants.

KANSAS STATE UNIVERSITY

KANSAS

Office of the Associate Dean
College of Veterinary Medicine
Veterinary Medical Center
Kansas State University
Trotter Hall
1700 Denison Avenue
Manhattan KS 66506-5601
Telephone: (913) 532-5660

Kansas State University in Manhattan, Kansas, is conveniently located 125 miles west of Kansas City near Interstate 70. With a population of about 45,000 including KSU, Manhattan is in an area surrounded by many historical points of interest in the rich farmland area of north central Kansas. Recreational activities abound in Manhattan and the surrounding area with fishing, boating, camping, and hunting among the favorites. Sporting events, theater, concerts, and excellent parks with swimming pools contribute to the many activities available. Kansans enjoy the four seasons, each of which brings its own special activities and events.

Kansas State University is on a beautiful 664 acre campus in northern Manhattan. Most buildings are constructed of native limestone. The College of Veterinary Medicine opened in 1905 and has developed into one of the finest in the United States. It is located on 80 acres just north of the main campus. The college is housed in three buildings constructed in the 1970s, and the facilities are ranked among the best of all veterinary colleges.

Application Information

Applications available: September 1; a preliminary application is available upon request.

Application deadline: January 15, 1996

Application fee: $20.00

Residency implications: priority is given to Kansas residents; minimum of 3 years' residence in Kansas is needed for eligibility for resident fees. Kansas contracts include: Alaska 0-3, Nebraska up to 25, North Dakota 0-2, Puerto Rico 0-3 (presently only 1 position funded), and Wyoming (open). Contract status is also determined by funding from the contracting state.

Kansas limits nonresident acceptances. At-large applicants may be from non-contract states.

(Veterinary Medical Colleges Application Service (VMCAS)): optional for all nonresidents.

63

Prerequisites for Admission

All science courses must have been taken within six years of the date of enrollment in the professional program. All preprofessional requirements must be graded, **not** "pass/fail" or "satisfactory/unsatisfactory."

If a course in Embryology is **not** offered at the school you are attending, Developmental Biology, Comparative Anatomy, Reproductive Physiology, or an advanced animal biology course may be substituted.

Course Requirements and Semester Hours

Expository writing I and II	6
Public speaking	2
Chemistry I and II	8
General organic chemistry, with laboratory	5
General biochemistry, with laboratory	5
Physics I and II	8
Principles of biology or general zoology	4
Mammalian embryology, with laboratory	4
Microbiology, with laboratory	4
Animal genetics or general genetics	3
Social sciences and/or humanities	12
Total:	61
Electives:	9
Total semester hours required:	70

Required undergraduate GPA: the required GPA is 2.8 on a 4-point scale in both the preprofessional requirements and the last 45 semester hours of undergraduate work. The most recent entering class had a mean GPA of 3.53.

Course completion deadline: prerequisite courses must be completed by the end of the spring term of the year in which admission is sought.

Standardized examinations: Graduate Record Examination General Test. The Class of 1999 had an average of 1095 (combining verbal and quantitative subtests). GRE scores should be sent to Kansas State University with Veterinary Medicine listed as department.

Additional Requirements and Considerations

Animal/veterinary work experience and knowledge
Names and addresses only, **not** letters, from:
  Academic or preprofessional advisor
  Personal acquaintance of more than five years
  A veterinarian with whom you have worked or are acquainted
Employment record

Summary of the Admission Procedure

A four-part admission procedure is used by Kansas State, including evaluation of grades, assessment of the application and narrative, review of evaluations, and a personal interview.

Timetable

Application deadline: January 15, 1996
Notification of interview: on-campus applicants, one week before interview; contract and at-large applicants, 3–4 weeks before interview.
Date interviews are held: on-campus (Kansas) applicants, October to early March; contract and at-large applicants, late January, February, early March.
Date acceptances mailed: March 15
Applicant's response date: April 15

Deposit (to hold place in class): $100.00 for Kansas and contract state residents, $250.00 for at-large students.

Deferments: may be granted by Admissions Committee for extraordinary circumstances.

Expenses for the 1995–96 Academic Year

Tuition and fees (subject to change)

Resident	$ 4,783.00
Nonresident	
Contract student	$ 4,783.00
Other nonresident	$15,733.00
Living expenses (estimated)	$ 6,000.00

1994–95 Admissions Summary

Listing below for "applicants" is the number interviewed. The number of applications processed was 717. At-large applicants were evaluated using the application and transcripts. Approximately four times the anticipated number to be accepted were interviewed.

	Number of Applicants Interviewed	Number of New Entrants Invited
In-state	82	50
Contract	58	30
Out-of-state (at-large)	107	27
Total:	247	107

School begins: August 17, 1995; first-year orientation on August 15–16.

Evaluation Criteria	% weight
Grades	50
Test scores (no specific weight assigned)	—
Animal/veterinary experience	7
Interview	32
References	6
Essay	3
Extracurricular activities	2

LOUISIANA STATE UNIVERSITY

Office of Veterinary Student Affairs
School of Veterinary Medicine
Louisiana State University
Baton Rouge LA 70803
Telephone: (504) 346-3155

The Louisiana State University campus is located in Baton Rouge, which has a population of more than 500,000 and is a major industrial city, a thriving port, and the state's capital. Since it is located on the Mississippi River, Baton Rouge was a target for domination by Spanish, French, and English settlers. The city bears the influence of all three cultures and offers a range of choices in everything from food to architectural design. Geographically, Baton Rouge is the center of south Louisiana's main cultural and recreational attractions. Equally distant from New Orleans and the fabled Cajun bayou country, there is an abundance of cultural and outdoor recreational activities. South Louisiana has a balmy climate that encourages lush vegetation and comfortable temperatures year round.

The campus encompasses more than 2,000 acres in the southern part of Baton Rouge and is bordered on the west by the Mississippi River. The Veterinary Medicine building, occupied in 1978, houses the academic departments, the veterinary library, and the Veterinary Teaching Hospital and clinics. The school is fully accredited by the American Veterinary Medical Association.

Application Information

Applications available: September

Application deadline: November 1

Application fee: $50.00

Residency implications: Louisiana contracts include Arkansas (9) and Puerto Rico (2). Louisiana accepts a limited number of highly qualified out-of-state applicants.

(Veterinary Medical Colleges Application Service (VMCAS)): required for all nonresidents.

Prerequisites for Admission

Course Requirements and Semester Hours

Biology	8
Microbiology	4
Physics	6
General chemistry	8
Organic chemistry	3
Biochemistry	3

Organic chemistry or biochemistry laboratory	1
English composition	6
Speech communication	3
Mathematics	5
Electives	<u>19</u>
Total Semester Credits:	66

Required undergraduate GPA: the minimum acceptable GPA for required course work is 2.5 on a 4-point scale. The mean GPA of the most recent entering class at the time of acceptance was 3.42.

Course completion deadline: prerequisite courses must be completed by the end of the spring term preceding matriculation.

Standardized examinations: Medical College Admission Test or *Graduate Record Examination* (general exam) is required. The latest acceptable test date is early fall of the year preceding application. The average GRE combined verbal and quantitative score was 1034 for the Class of 1999.

Additional Requirements and Considerations

Animal/veterinary work experience
Motivation, maturity
Demonstrated communication skills
Breadth of interests

Summary of Admission Procedure

The approximate components of the evaluation scoring are:
Objective evaluation:

GPA required courses	32%
GPA last 45 hours	20%
MCAT or GRE	18%

Subjective evaluation:

File review	16%
Personal interview	10%
Committee evaluation	4%

Timetable

Application deadline: November 1
Notification of interview: March 1
Date interviews are held: March 15
Date acceptances mailed: April
Applicant's response date: April 15

Deposit (to hold place in class): nonresident $500.00

Deferments: considered

Expenses for the 1995–96 Academic Year

Tuition and fees (estimated)

Resident	$ 4,458.00
Nonresident	
Contract student	$ 4,458.00
Other nonresident	$14,608.00

Other expenses (estimated)

Board	$ 1,750.00
Room	$ 1,750.00
Books, supplies	$ 1,250.00
Personal	$ 2,000.00

1994–95 Admissions Summary

	Number of Applicants	Number of New Entrants
In-state	105	60
Contract	55	10
Out-of-state	210	10
Total:	370	80

School begins: August 24, 1995

Evaluation Criteria

	% weight
Grades	52
Test scores	18
Animal/veterinary experience, references, essay	16
Interview	10

Special Programs

A limited number of exchange students from other schools of veterinary medicine can be accommodated for short periods of clinical work in the final year.

MICHIGAN STATE UNIVERSITY

MICHIGAN

Admissions Office
College of Veterinary Medicine
A-126 East Fee Hall
Michigan State University
East Lansing MI 48824-1316
Telephone: (517) 353-9793
Fax: (517) 432-2391

Michigan State University's campus is bordered by the city of East Lansing, which offers sidewalk cafes, restaurants, shops, and convenient mass transit. The campus is traversed by the Red Cedar River and has many miles of bike paths and walkways. This park-like setting provides an ideal venue in which MSU's 41,000 students may enjoy outdoor concerts and plays, canoeing, and cross-country skiing. North of the river is the older part of campus. The ivy-covered buildings, some built before the Civil War and listed on the National Register of Historic Places, house five colleges, the student union, and ten residence halls. South of the river are more recent additions to the campus, such as the Wharton Center for Performing Arts, the Jack Breslin Student Events Center and several intramural sports facilities.

The college is a national leader in state-of-the-art technology and facilities. A lecture hall is equipped with a computer at each of the 116 work stations. These computers are part of a network that links all parts of the Veterinary Medical Center (VMC) and allows instructors to receive immediate feedback on how well students understand the lecture material. The Veterinary Teaching Hospital has one of the largest caseloads in the country. Outstanding faculty are involved in teaching veterinary students, providing patient treatment and diagnostic services, and conducting veterinary research.

Application Information

Applications available: July 1

Application deadline: early decision, October 15; regular, November 1

Application fee: $65.00

Residency implications: priority is given to Michigan residents. Michigan State gives equal consideration to residents of any other state in the United States and encourages out-of-state residents to apply. Michigan State has no contractual agreements.

(Veterinary Medical Colleges Application Service (VMCAS)): required for all residents and nonresidents.

Prerequisites for Admission

To be eligible for admission to the professional program in veterinary medicine, the following courses must be completed prior to the fall matriculation.

Course Requirements and Semester Hours (quarter hour equivalent)

General Education
English composition, literature, speech, etc.	3
Social and behavioral sciences	6
Humanities	6

Mathematics, and Biological and Physical Sciences
General inorganic chemistry, with laboratory	3
Organic chemistry, with laboratory	6
Basic biochemistry	4
General biology, with laboratory	6
College algebra and trigonometry	3
Introductory physics, with laboratory	8

Required undergraduate GPA: none; the mean cumulative GPA for the last selected class was 3.488 on a 4.0 scale.

Course completion deadline: prerequisite courses must be completed by matriculation.

Standardized examinations: **all** applicants are required to take **either** the MCAT **or** the GRE. Date of oldest acceptable test scores is September 1990.

Medical College Admission Test (MCAT). For applicants to the Class of 2000, the latest acceptable test scores are those of the August 1995 exam. The average MCAT scores for the class entering in 1995 were: verbal 9.13, physical sciences 8.25, and biological sciences 8.05.

Graduate Record Examination (GRE). For applicants to the Class of 2000, the latest acceptable test scores are those of the October 14, 1995 exam. For the class entering in 1995, average GRE scores were: verbal 540, quantitative 619, and analytical 663.

Additional Requirements and Considerations

Extracurricular and/or community service activities
Veterinary related experience
Evaluations
  Veterinarian
  Applicant's choice (two)
  Academic advisor (if graduate student)

Summary of Admission Procedure

There are two phases to Michigan State's admission process, consisting of an academic review and an interview with a pre-interview extemporaneous composition.

Timetable

Application deadline: early decision, October 15; regular, November 1
Notification of interview: February

Date interviews are held: during March
Date acceptances mailed: April 1
Applicant's response date: April 15

Deposit (to hold place in class): none at this time; a proposed amount is under consideration.

Deferments: granted only for one year under extreme circumstances.

Expenses for the 1994–95 Academic Year

The Board of Trustees reserves the right to increase figures for the tuition and fees category, if necessary.

Tuition and fees
Resident	$ 9,550.00
Nonresident	$19,676.00
Books, room and board, etc. (estimated)	$ 6,952.00

1994–95 Admissions Summary

	Number of Applicants	Number (as of 4-28-95) selected for new class
In-state	209	80
Out-of-state	352	20
Total:	561	100

School begins: August 28, 1995

Special Admissions Programs

Early Decision Option: The College of Veterinary Medicine includes in its regular admission cycle an early decision option for qualified students. Using this procedure, the committee selects no more than 10 percent of the veterinary class that matriculates in September. Any applicant not selected through the early decision option automatically will be reconsidered through the regular admission process. Applicants must have completed all of the credits in chemistry, general physics, general biology, college algebra and trigonometry, arts and humanities, social science, and English, referenced above, at the time they submit an application for admission under the early decision option. In addition, standardized admission test scores must be submitted on or before the application deadline date. The application deadline is October 15, and students who are admitted under this option will be notified by November 15.

Preveterinary Scholars Enrichment Program: The College of Veterinary Medicine offers a Preveterinary Scholars Enrichment Program to high-achieving students enrolling in the Preveterinary Program at MSU. In this special program, students participate in activities normally limited to those admitted to the four-year professional veterinary medical program. Program components include mentoring assignments with CVM faculty and students and participation in veterinary student organizations and activities.

The intent of the program is to reinforce and nurture the interest of high-ability students by providing breadth of exposure to career opportunities in the veterinary profession, active participation in the veterinary curriculum and its co-curricular activities, and enhancement of credentials for admission to the DVM program through enriched veterinary-animal experience and animal exposure.

Eligibility criteria include:
• Minimum high school GPA of 3.5
• Top 10 percent of high school graduating class
• Minimum ACT composite of 30 and/or minimum SAT total of 1200
• Admission to the MSU Preveterinary Program

All students who have been admitted to MSU and meet the eligibility criteria receive an invitation to participate in the program. This program is currently under review and is subject to change.

Automatic Admission Option: Preveterinary Scholars Enrichment Program students who commit themselves to completion of a bachelor's degree may apply for automatic admission to the DVM program. The Committee on Admissions selects candidates for the Automatic Admission Option. Eligibility criteria include:

• Completion of at least one year of study at MSU
• Minimum 3.0 cumulative GPA and minimum 3.25 preveterinary science GPA
• Projected completion plan for a bachelor's degree
• Satisfactory performance on the following regular DVM program admission criteria: GRE/MCAT score, interview, autobiography, confidential evaluations, and extracurricular activities and achievements
• Minimum of 240 hours or documented veterinary-related animal experience
• Satisfactory completion of at least 10 credits in advanced (300-level or above) or diverse courses not included in the preveterinary requirements
• Satisfactory evaluation by a faculty mentor and preveterinary adviser

The College of Veterinary Medicine at Michigan State University reserves the right to evaluate and modify its admissions requirements procedures and selection criteria each year. MSU reserves the right to make changes in fees, tuition, and housing rates.

UNIVERSITY OF MINNESOTA

Office of Student Affairs and Admissions
College of Veterinary Medicine
University of Minnesota
460 VTH
1365 Gortner Avenue
St. Paul MN 55108
Telephone: (612) 624-4747

The University of Minnesota's College of Veterinary Medicine is located on the 540-acre St. Paul campus. Students enjoy a small-campus atmosphere as well as the academic, cultural, social, and recreational opportunities of a major university and large metropolitan area. Cultural life includes world-renowned institutions and a rich local mix of theatre, music, and arts organizations. The Twin Cities also house the state capital and the headquarters of many diverse major corporations. Minneapolis and St. Paul consistently rank near the top on quality-of-life and residential satisfaction ratings.

The College of Veterinary Medicine blends cornfields with biotechnology and cow barns with state-of-the-art diagnostic laboratories. The college provides contemporary facilities such as Lewis Hospital for Companion Animals, built in 1983, which is one of the most modern, well-equipped veterinary teaching hospitals in the country, and the Raptor Center, which in 1988 became the world's first facility designed specifically for birds of prey. The educational opportunities extend beyond the campus to include farms throughout Minnesota, the Minnesota Zoo, and even Uruguay and Morocco. Students are given opportunities to learn about the practice of contemporary veterinary medicine through preceptorships, clinical rotations, and first-hand experiences with practitioners.

Application Information

Applications available: July

Application deadline: November 15

Application fee: $50.00

Residency implications: first priority is given to Minnesota residents, minority applicants, and residents of states/provinces with which reciprocity agreement exists (North Dakota, South Dakota, Manitoba). Residents of other states are encouraged to apply.

(Veterinary Medical Colleges Application Service (VMCAS)): required for all residents and nonresidents.

Beginning in fall 1996, admission to the University of Minnesota will be part of the National VMCAS application system. In addition to the National Application, a supplemental application from the University of Minnesota will be required of all applicants.

Prerequisites for Admission

Course Requirements and Quarter Hours

Freshman English, communication	8
Mathematics	4
Chemistry (must include laboratory)	
General inorganic	12
General organic*	10
Biology (must include laboratory)	4
Zoology/animal biology (must include laboratory)	4
Physics (must include laboratory)	10-15
Biochemistry	4
Genetics	4
Microbiology (must include laboratory)	4
Liberal Education	16-20

* Two quarters with one laboratory or one semester with laboratory

Other Courses   16-20 credits

A minimum of four courses from the following areas of study: anthropology, art, economics, geography, history, humanities, literature (including foreign language literature), music, political science, psychology, public speaking or small group (interpersonal) communication, social science, sociology, theater.

No more than two courses can be from the same area of study.

Required undergraduate GPA: no minimum required. The Class of 1999 had a mean GPA of 3.50 (on a 4-point scale) for required courses and 3.60 for the last 60 quarter-hour or 45 semester-hour credits of coursework prior to admission.

Course completion deadline: prerequisite courses must be completed by the end of the spring term (not later than June 15) of the academic year in which application is made.

Standardized examinations: Graduate Record Examination: the verbal, quantitative, and analytical portions are required, and results must be received by March 1. The mean combined score for the three tests for the class entering in autumn 1995 was 1860.

Summary of Admission Procedure

The University of Minnesota ranks applicants on the basis of a 100-point scale. Applicants should note that selection criteria and point system are subject to change. For fall 1995 admission these criteria are:

Objective measures of educational background	*70 points*
1. GPA in required courses	20 points

2. GPA in recent courses   20 points
3. Graduate Record Examination   30 points

Subjective measures of personal experience   *30 points*
    Animal/veterinary knowledge, experience, and interest
    Employment record
    Communication skills
    Extracurricular and/or community service activities
    Leadership abilities

Timetable

Application deadline: November 15
Date acceptances mailed: April 15 or earlier
Applicant's response date: within one month of admissions offer

Deposit (to hold place in class): $100.00 (Minnesota, South Dakota, and North Dakota residents) and $250.00 (nonresidents)

Deferments: can be requested for special circumstances that warrant a 1-year delay in admission. Nine deferments were granted for current entering class.

Expenses for the 1995–96 Academic Year

Tuition and fees (three quarters)
Residents and Reciprocity $ 8,385.00
Nonresidents $13,162.00

Living expenses (estimated) $3,500-$5,500
    (excludes books and supplies)

Fall 1995 Admissions Summary

The figures for new entrants expected includes students taking delayed admission from the previous year.

	Number of Applicants	Number of New Entrants
In-state	140	58
Reciprocity	30	3
Out-of-state	320	15
Total:	490	76

School begins: September 22, 1995

Evaluation Criteria

	% weight
Grades	40
Test scores	30
Animal/veterinary experience	15
References	Yes
Essay	Yes
Maturity/reliability	15

MISSISSIPPI STATE UNIVERSITY

College of Veterinary Medicine
Mississippi State University
P.O. Box 9825
Mississippi State MS 39762
Telephone: (601) 325-1129

Mississippi State University is located in Starkville (population 18,000). The university has an enrollment of about 13,500. Places of historical interest are prevalent throughout the area. Temperatures are moderate, ranging from the 40s in January to the 90s in July. Air service to the area is fifteen minutes away with daily flights that connect with Memphis, Atlanta, and Nashville.

Each class in the College of Veterinary Medicine has 48 students. The curriculum is divided into four phases and involves two primary learning environments: a problem-based learning mode in which students learn basic and clinical sciences through exposure to simulated cases in small group settings, and an experiential mode in which students are rotated through each functional area of the veterinary teaching hospital assisting in the primary diagnosis and care of animal patients. Significant elective opportunities allow students the flexibility to focus study by species, species group, or discipline. A college-wide computer network coupled with a student computer requirement facilitates student communication and access to up-to-date veterinary medical information. Visitors are welcome at the College of Veterinary Medicine and are invited to telephone [601-325-1129] the Office of Student Planning and Development. The college suggests calling two weeks ahead of the proposed visit so that an appointment may be scheduled.

Application Information

Applications available: July 15

Application deadline: November 1

Application fee supplement: $25.00

Residency implications: Mississippi accepts 19 at-large students.

(Veterinary Medical Colleges Application Service (VMCAS)): required for all residents and nonresidents.

Prerequisites for Admission

Science and math courses must be on the level of those required for preveterinary, predentistry, or science majors and must be completed within six calendar years prior to anticipated date of enrollment.

Course Requirements and Semester Hours

Communication	
English composition	6
Oral communication	3
Biological sciences, with laboratories: microbiology, vertebrate zoology, cell biology, genetics	14
Physical sciences, with laboratories: inorganic chemistry, organic chemistry, biochemistry, physics	18
Mathematics	
College algebra, analytic geometry, trigonometry, calculus, finite mathematics, or statistics	6
Nutrition	3-5
Humanities, fine arts, and social and behavioral sciences	<u>15</u>
Total Semester Hour Credits:	67

Required undergraduate GPA: on a 4-point scale, a minimum GPA of 2.8. The required prerequisite science GPA is 3.00. The Class of 1997 had an average GPA of 3.30.

Course completion deadline: prerequisites must be completed before June 1 prior to matriculation.

Standardized examinations: VCAT is required.

Additional Requirements and Considerations

Evaluation of written application
Confidential evaluations
Interview (by invitation on a competitive basis)

Summary of Admissions Procedure

Timetable

Application deadline: November 1
Notification of interview: February
Date interviews are held: late February–early March
Date acceptances mailed: late March
Applicant's response date: April 15

Deposit (to hold place in class): $250.00 (nonrefundable) due with letter of acceptance. The deposit is applied to summer tuition.

Deferments: requests are considered on an individual basis.

Expenses for the 1995–96 Academic Year

Tuition and fees (first-year class entering June 1994)	
Tuition	$ 4,500.00
* Professional Education Fee	$10,500.00
Activities Fee	$ 715.00
Computer, books, and supplies (approximate)	$ 3,210.00

1994–95 Admissions Summary

	Number of Applicants	Number of New Entrants
In-state	64	30
Out-of-state	122	19
Total:	186	49

School begins: May 29, 1995

Evaluation Criteria

* Assessment of the Professional Education Fee is based upon participation in the Mississippi tax system and state of legal residency is not a factor.

	% weight
Grades	50
VCAT scores	10
Interview; animal/veterinary experience	25
References	5
Application (includes essay)	10

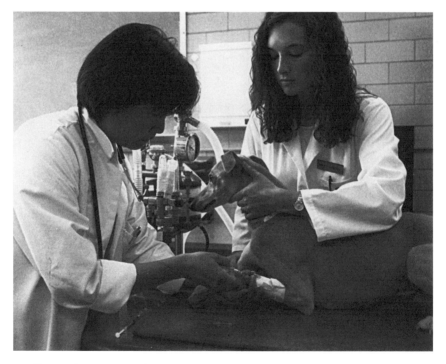

Small animal clinician and senior student induce anesthesia in order to take cervical radiographs of Mighty Mite at the Purdue University School of Veterinary Medicine's Veterinary Teaching Hospital.

UNIVERSITY OF MISSOURI

Office of Academic Affairs
College of Veterinary Medicine
W203 Veterinary Medicine Building
University of Missouri-Columbia
Columbia MO 65211
Telephone: (314) 882-3554

The University of Missouri with its 23,000 students is located in Columbia, Missouri. The city of 60,000 is situated 125 miles from either St. Louis or Kansas City and about 100 miles north of the Missouri Ozarks. Columbia is a city of three colleges, some light industry, major insurance companies, and a number of health-related facilities including a medical school, a Veteran's Hospital, and a veterinary medical college.

The city and campus provide many cultural activities and sporting events. Living conditions are good and housing is plentiful. Many students elect to live in the country, which is only a short distance from the College of Veterinary Medicine. Hunting for turkey, deer, quail, and other game is available. Fishing throughout the state ranges from farm ponds to large lakes and clear running streams. The climate is generally mild, although some parts of the summer are hot and humid. Winter may have a few days of snow or ice.

Application Information

Applications available: July 1 to October 15

Application deadline: November 1

Application fee: $50.00

Residency implications: first priority is given to Missouri residents; second priority is given to residents of states without an accredited school of veterinary medicine; finally, residents of states with a school of veterinary medicine are considered.

Prerequisites for Admission

Course Requirements and Semester Hours

English or communication	6
College algebra or more advanced mathematics	3
Inorganic chemistry	8
Organic chemistry (with laboratory)	5
Physics	5

Biological science	10
Social sciences or humanities	10
Animal or human nutrition, requires chemistry prerequisite	3
Electives	8
Biochemistry (without laboratory), requires organic chemistry prerequisite	3

Required undergraduate GPA: a cumulative GPA of 2.50 or more on a 4-point scale is required for Missouri residents. Out-of-state residents must have a cumulative GPA of 3.0 or more. The most recent entering class had a mean GPA of 3.4 at the time of acceptance.

Course completion deadline: prerequisite courses must be completed by the end of the winter semester or spring quarter of the year of entry.

Standardized examinations: Veterinary College Admission Test is required. Scores must be received by the Admissions Office by February 1. The last entering class had a mean score of 56.

(Veterinary Medical Colleges Application Service (VMCAS)): no participation.

Additional Requirements and Considerations

Animal/veterinary experience
Recommendations/evaluations
  Employer
  Academic advisors
  Veterinarians
Extracurricular and/or community service activities
Essays
  Animal experience
  Explanation of choice of veterinary medicine as a profession
Employment history

Summary of Admission Procedure

The admission process at the University of Missouri consists of a file review and may include a personal interview.

Timetable

Application deadline: November 1
Notification of interview: February and March
Date interviews are held: February, March
Date acceptances mailed: by April 15
Applicant's response date: residents, two weeks; nonresidents, April 15

Deposit (to hold place in class): $100.00 for Missouri residents; $250.00 for non-Missouri residents.

Deferments: each is considered individually by the admissions committee.

Expenses for the 1995–96 Academic Year

The estimated total cost for a single, off-campus Missouri resident is $20,700.00, including the following:

Tuition and fees
Resident $ 8,514.00
Nonresident
  Other nonresident $16,463.00

Living expenses $12,186.00

1993–94 Admissions Summary

	Number of Applicants	Number of New Entrants
In-state	127	56
Out-of-state	170	8
Total:	297	64

School begins: August 17, 1995

Evaluation Criteria

	% weight
Grades	50
Test scores	5
Animal/veterinary experience	15
Interview	10
References	10
Essay	10

Special Programs

The College of Veterinary Medicine at the University of Missouri has a unique clinical block system which involves all of the last two years of the four-year curriculum. Instruction is centered around patient care, case studies, and problem-based learning. There are seven required blocks; each are eight weeks long. Three eight-week blocks are free to use as continuing education within the college, to gather practical experience outside the college, or to use as vacation. Free blocks may occur any month of the year.

Special Admissions Programs

Missouri has scholarships available for the top two scoring applicants, for ethnic minorities, and for disadvantaged students enrolling in the College of Veterinary Medicine.

Preveterinary Medicine Scholars Program: This program guarantees acceptance into the MU College of Veterinary Medicine, upon satisfactory completion of the undergraduate requirements at the University of Missouri. Eligibility requires a high school senior or MU freshman to have a composite ACT score of at least 30, or an equivalent SAT score. Eligible applicants will be interviewed and a satisfactory score must be achieved to become a Pre-Vet Med Scholar. Selected faculty in the College of Veterinary Medicine will be assigned as mentors to Scholars. Scholars receive priority consideration for part-time employment in the college. For more information, contact the Associate Dean for Academic Affairs.

NORTH CAROLINA STATE UNIVERSITY

Office of Admissions
College of Veterinary Medicine
4700 Hillsborough Street
North Carolina State University
Raleigh NC 27606
Telephone: (919) 829-4205

The North Carolina College of Veterinary Medicine is located in Raleigh, which has a population of more than 212,000. The sandy shores of North Carolina's beautiful coastline are a short ride to the east, and the Great Smoky mountains are to the west. The climate includes mild winters and warm summers.

The College of Veterinary Medicine opened in the fall of 1981 and occupies more than 260,000 square feet, including a teaching hospital, classrooms, animal wards, research and teaching laboratories, and an audiovisual area. The college has 120 faculty members and capacity for 288 students with training for interns, residents, and special students. Graduates are trained to practice large or small animal medicine.

Application Information

Applications available: July

Application deadline: November 1

Application fee: see VMCAS

Residency implications: priority is given to North Carolina residents. There are approximately 12 nonresident positions.

(Veterinary Medical Colleges Application Service (VMCAS)): required for all residents and nonresidents.

Prerequisites for Admission

Course Requirements and Semester Hours

English composition, rhetoric, and reading	6
Analytic geometry and calculus A	4
or, introduction to calculus	4
Introduction to statistics	3
General physics	8
General chemistry I	4
Principles of chemistry	4
Organic chemistry I, II	8

General biology	4
Principles of genetics	4
General microbiology	4
Elementary biochemistry	3
Animal or human nutrition	3/4
Social sciences and the humanities (each)	6

Course completion deadline: only two courses may be pending completion in the spring semester, and both must be completed (with transcript evidence) by the end of the spring semester prior to matriculation. Pending courses may not be completed in summer sessions.

Standardized examinations: no examination is required.

Additional Requirements and Considerations

Animal/veterinary knowledge, experience, and motivation
Autobiography
Recommendations/evaluations by three persons of the applicant's choice (at least one evaluator must be a veterinarian unrelated to the applicant)
Extracurricular activities

Summary of Admission Procedure

Selection for admission at North Carolina State University is a two-phase process:

Objective score: 55% of total
    Required course GPA
    Cumulative GPA
    Collegiate experiences
Subjective score: 45% of total
    Interview

Timetable

Application deadline: November 1
Notification of interview: second week in February
Date interviews are held: university spring break in March
Date acceptances mailed: third week in March
Applicant's response date: April 15

Deposit (to hold place in class): $250.00, applied to fall tuition; nonrefundable on July 1.

Deferments: are considered for one year only, subject to Admissions Committee approval.

Expenses for the 1994–95 Academic Year

Tuition and fees	
Resident	$ 2,391.00
Nonresident	$15,941.00
Books and immunizations (all students)	$ 620.00
Living expenses (estimated)	$ 7,450.00

1994–95 Admissions Summary

	Number of Applicants	*Number of New Entrants*
In-state	216	64
Out-of-state	<u>282</u>	<u>14</u>
Total:	498	78

School begins: August 24, 1995

Evaluation Criteria	*% weight*
Grades	50
Interview	45
Collegiate experience, degrees held	5

Special Admissions Programs

A combined D.V.M./Ph.D. program is available. Candidates must apply to both to be accepted.

An early admissions option for students focusing on swine or poultry medicine is offered in concert with the College of Agriculture and Life Sciences (North Carolina residents only).

Ohio State University

Chairperson, Admissions Committee
College of Veterinary Medicine
0004 Veterinary Hospital
601 Tharp Street
Columbus OH 43210
Telephone: (614) 292-8831
Fax: (614) 262-6989

Ohio State University is located in Columbus, the capital of Ohio. Columbus is a congregation of cities and villages with a sense of history and a friendly atmosphere. The third ranking center of scientific and technological research and data dissemination in the United States, the city offers fine arts, restaurants, sports, architecture, nature, community festivals, churches, and other areas of interest.

The Ohio State University is one of the nation's leading academic centers with a sprawling campus straddling the Olentangy River. The campus consists of thousands of acres, hundreds of buildings, more than 15,000 faculty and staff, and more than 56,000 students. The veterinary college is the third oldest in the United States and is one of the largest veterinary colleges in North America. The patient load is one of the highest in the country and farmlands can be accessed ten miles from campus. The faculty members have diverse academic and research activities and 85 percent of the clinical teaching faculty are board certified. The academic curriculum is a four-year program that blends some clinical experience into the first two years, while the last two years are mostly clinical.

Application Information

Applications available: August 1

Application deadline: November 1

Application fee: $30.00

Residency implications: priority is given to Ohio residents. Ohio contracts include: Nevada 1–2, New Jersey 4, Puerto Rico 1, and West Virginia 5. Ohio will consider qualified nonresident students.

(Veterinary Medical Colleges Application Service (VMCAS)): no participation.

Prerequisites for Admission

For the humanities and social sciences requirement, students are encouraged to elect the courses required for the Bachelor of Science curriculum. Courses in communication, journalism, sociology, economics, and animal behavior are strongly recommended.

Students enrolled in the preveterinary medicine curriculum are encouraged to take electives that will provide a well-rounded education in addition to those biological sciences preparatory to the veterinary medical curriculum.

Course Requirements and Quarter Hours

English	5
General chemistry	15
Organic chemistry	6
Biochemistry	5
Biology	10
Genetics	5
Microbiology	10
Mathematics (algebra and trigonometry)	5
General physics	10
Humanities and social sciences	20
Electives	10
Total Quarter Hour Credits:	101

Required undergraduate GPA: the minimum acceptable GPA for Ohio residents is 2.7; however, students with 3.0 average or above will be given preferential consideration. The minimum acceptable GPA for contract-state residents is 3.0 and for nonresidents is 3.4 (on a 4-point scale). An undergraduate degree is not a requirement. The Ohio State University calculates a single, comprehensive GPA, which will include grades from all college level work (both graduate and undergraduate) completed by the applicant.

Course completion deadline: prerequisite courses must be completed by the end of the spring semester or winter quarter following submission of the application. This is the spring semester or winter quarter preceding the first quarter of matriculation in the professional curriculum. Failure to satisfactorily complete prerequisites will result in automatic loss of a candidate's seat in the class.

Graduate students: when applying to the College of Veterinary Medicine, graduate students must have a letter from their advisor releasing them from their graduate program if accepted into the veterinary medicine program.

Standardized examinations: the Ohio State University requires that scores from **one** of the following standardized examinations be submitted:

Graduate Record Examination: minimum acceptable score 1500 total of all three subtests. The Class of 1998 average GRE total was 1752.
Medical College Admission Test: minimum acceptable score 24 total; score O–T on essay portion (new MCAT). The Class of 1998 MCAT average was 39.
Veterinary College Admission Test: minimum acceptable score 50th percentile. The Class of 1998 average was at the 54th percentile.

Scores must not be older than five years prior to the application year. The oldest acceptable scores are those from 1990. The latest acceptable test date for applicants to the Class of 1999 is October 1995.

Additional Requirements and Considerations

Academic improvement/difficulty
Personal/evaluations

Involvement in community affairs
Communication/interpersonal skills
Initiative/leadership
Attitude/motivation/judgment
Work record/financial responsibility
Social and personal support systems
Comprehension of veterinary medical/animal work experience
Comparative medical experience

Summary of Admission Procedure

Preferred applicants are interviewed and evaluated by members of the Admissions Committee. Those given the highest overall evaluation are selected for the entering class.

Timetable

Application deadline: November 1
Notification of interview: students with acceptable GPA and test score will be invited for an interview.
Date interviews are held: all interviews are held between November and March (residents of Nevada and West Virginia will be interviewed in their home states).
Date acceptances mailed: March 15
Applicant's response date: residents, 10 days; contract and nonresidents by April 15.

Deposit (to hold place in class): $25.00 for Ohio residents; $300.00 for contract and nonresident applicants.

Deferments: not considered.

Expenses for the 1995–96 Academic Year

Tuition and fees
Resident $ 7,371.00
Nonresident* $22,566.00

* Contract students are assessed the nonresident tuition and fees. The contract state subsidy is subtracted from that tuition and the student pays the balance due. In 1993-94, the contract student's portion of the tuition and fees averaged $7,814.00.

Books, instruments, etc. (for one year) $ 1,154.00
Health insurance $ 510.00

Living expenses (estimated; includes resident tuition)
Single $ 9,826.00
Married $12,826.00

1995–96 Admissions Summary

	Number of Applicants	Number of New Entrants
In-state	246	97
Contract	53	10
Out-of-state	124	26
Total:	423	133

School begins: September 22, 1995; orientation, September 18–19.

Evaluation Criteria

	% weight
Grades	40
Test scores	5
Interview**	55

** The academic interview covers subjective areas such as academic improvement versus difficulty, communication/interpersonal skills, involvement in social and community activities, social and personal support systems, work record/financial responsibility, motivation and commitment to veterinary medicine, comprehension of veterinary medicine, knowledge of and/or exposure to animals, and references.

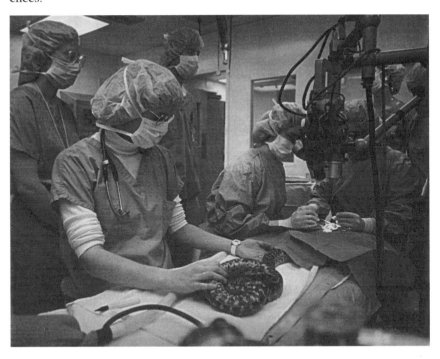

As part of their exotic pet practice, veterinary ophthalmologists are performing eye surgery on an anesthesized snake at the small animal hospital of The Ohio State University College of Veterinary Medicine.

PHOTO BY JOHN J. SWARTZ

OKLAHOMA STATE UNIVERSITY

OKLAHOMA

Coordinator of Admissions
College of Veterinary Medicine
Stillwater OK 74078-0353
Telephone: (405) 744-6653

Oklahoma State University is located in Stillwater, which has a population of about 38,000. Stillwater is in north central Oklahoma about sixty-five miles from Oklahoma City and sixty-nine miles from Tulsa. The campus is exceptionally beautiful with modified Georgian-style architecture in the new buildings. It encompasses 840 acres and 62 major academic buildings.

Three major buildings form the veterinary medicine complex. The oldest, Veterinary Medicine, was recently renovated to provide the William E. Brock Memorial Library and Learning Center, as well as first- and second-year classrooms. The Boren Veterinary Medical Teaching Hospital provides the most modern facilities for both academic and clinical instruction for third- and fourth-year students. Completing the triad is the Oklahoma Animal Disease Laboratory, which provides both teaching resources and services to Oklahoma agriculture and industry. The College of Veterinary Medicine is fully accredited by the American Veterinary Medical Association. Faculty members in the four academic departments share responsibility for the curriculum. These departments are Veterinary Medicine and Surgery; Veterinary Pathology; Veterinary Parasitology, Microbiology and Public Health; and Physiological Sciences. The latter three departments also offer graduate programs for the Master of Science and Doctor of Philosophy degrees.

Application Information

Applications available: July 1

Application deadline: December 1

Application Fee: See VMCAS

Residency implications: priority is given to Oklahoma residents. Nonresidents may apply and Oklahoma State could admit up to 11 first-time nonresident students to the class entering in fall 1995, but this is subject to change without further notice.

(Veterinary Medical Colleges Application Service (VMCAS)): required for all residents and nonresidents.

Prerequisites for Admission

The following is strongly recommended: courses taken in addition to those required for admission should be chosen to fulfill requirements leading to a baccalaureate degree in the event the applicant is not admitted to the College of Veterinary Medicine.

The semester-hour requirements listed below are the **minimum** required for admission to the program.

Course Requirements and Semester Hours

English composition	6
English elective	2
General chemistry	8
Organic chemistry	8
Biochemistry	3
Physics	8
Mathematics	3
Zoology	4
Biological science elective	3
Microbiology	4
Genetics	3
Humanities or social sciences	6
Electives (science or business)	2
Total Semester Hour Credits:	60

Required undergraduate GPA: a minimum GPA of 2.8 on a 4-point scale is required in prerequisite courses. The mean cumulative GPA of the Class of 1999 was 3.43.

Alternative admissions: in the interest of social justice and of cultural diversity, the Oklahoma State Regents for Higher Education permit the College to accept up to 15% of a beginning class who do not meet minimum requirements. Limited to Oklahoma residents.

Course completion deadline: prerequisite courses must be completed by the end of the spring semester just prior to anticipated matriculation.

Standardized examinations: Graduate Record Examination, General Test, and Biology Subject Test required. The latest acceptable test date for applicants to the Class of 1999 is October 1995. Earliest acceptable test date is June, 1990.

The Class of 1999 had mean scores of 483 (verbal), 564 (quantitative), 583 (analytical), and 564 (biology).

Additional Requirements and Considerations

Evidence of motivation over an extended period of time
Animal/veterinary work experience
Amount of undergraduate education completed
Personal recommendations/evaluations
Demonstrated leadership and interpersonal skills
All science courses must have been taken within the past eight years.

Summary of Admission Procedure

The admission procedure at Oklahoma State consists of evaluation of both academic and nonacademic criteria. The Admissions Committee considers all factors in the applicant's file, but the following are especially important: academic ability; familiarity with the profession and sincerity of interest; recommendations; GRE scores; extracurricular activities; character, personality, and general fitness and adaptability for a career in veterinary medicine. The committee selects those applicants considered most capable of excelling as veterinary medical students and who possess the greatest potential for success in veterinary medicine.

Timetable

Application deadline: November 1
Notification of interview: early March
Date interviews are held: March
Date acceptances mailed: March
Applicant's response date: April 15

Deposit (to hold place in class): resident, $100.00; nonresident, $500.00; not refundable.

Deferments: to complete graduate degree, deferments are considered.

Expenses for the 1995–96 Academic Year*

Basic academic expenses per semester for 20 hours are approximate as given below (stated fees are current for 1993-94):

Resident
Enrollment fee	$2,125.00
Activities fee ($2.86/cr. hr.)	57.20
Facilities fee ($4.30/cr. hr.) max.	68.80
Health Service fee	46.00
Health Risk Assessment fee (new students)	20.00
Library Automation fee ($1.50/cr. hr.)	30.00
O'Collegian fee	2.00
Resident total	$2,349.00

Nonresident
Tuition	$3,921.50
Nonresident total	$6,270.50

* Fees and tuition are set in late summer by the Oklahoma State Regents for Higher Education. Prospective applicants should telephone the college for up-to-date estimates.

1994–95 Admissions Summary

	Number of Applicants	Number of New Entrants
In-state	124	60
Out-of-state	287	11
Total:	411	71

O KLAHOMA

School begins: August 21, 1995

Evaluation Criteria

	% weight
Required course GPA	25
Cumulative GPA	25
Test scores (GRE + Biology)	25
Animal/veterinary experience, interview, references	25

OREGON STATE UNIVERSITY

OREGON

Office of the Dean
College of Veterinary Medicine
Oregon State University
Magruder Hall 200
Corvallis OR 97331-4801
Telephone: (503) 737-2098
Fax: (503) 737-4245

At Oregon State University's College of Veterinary Medicine, students learn the skills to treat and prevent animal diseases through a rigorous course of study taught by a dedicated faculty.

The city of Corvallis, home of OSU, is a modern city of 49,000 that boasts theaters and parks, an art center and shopping malls, and public transportation and bicycle paths to every corner of the community. Life in Corvallis includes lectures, concerts, theater productions, films, and exhibits through the university. Students can explore the great outdoors just over an hour away by car at the spectacular Oregon coast, the snow-capped Oregon Cascades, and the city of Portland. In the heart of the agriculturally rich Willamette River Valley, Corvallis enjoys colorful and crisp autumns, mild and rainy winters, warm and flowering springs, and hot and dry summers.

Each year, 36 students from Oregon and the Western Regional Compact states (Alaska, Arizona, Hawaii, Montana, Nevada, New Mexico, North Dakota, Utah, and Wyoming) enter the College of Veterinary Medicine and take their first year of professional study at OSU. They then transfer to Washington State University in Pullman for the second year and half of the third year of study, then return to Corvallis to complete their year and take their fourth and final year of professional instruction. The small class size and the split approach to veterinary medical education, unique in the United States, helps to provide the students with an excellent veterinary education.

Application Information

Applications available: July 1

Application deadline: November 1

Application fee: see VMCAS

Residency requirements: only Oregon residents and WICHE students are eligible for resident fees.

(Veterinary Medical Colleges Application Service (VMCAS)): required for all residents and nonresidents.

93

Prerequisites for Admission

Course Requirements	Required Hours
Chemistry	One-year sequence of inorganic including laboratory; one semester or two-quarter sequence of organic including laboratory; and one upper division biochemistry course
Mathematics	Sufficient to meet the prerequisite for physics (at least college-level algebra)
Physics	One quarter or one semester of college physics
Zoology or biology	One-year sequence
Genetics	One quarter or one semester

Total minimum number of credits required: 90 quarter credits

Required undergraduate GPA: overall GPA must be at least 3.00 or the last two years must be at least 3.00. The mean overall GPA for the class entering in fall of 1995 was 3.42.

Course completion deadline: prerequisite courses must be completed by June 15 prior to entry.

Standardized examinations: candidates for admission are required to take the *Graduate Record Examination* (GRE); the latest acceptable test date for applicants to the Class of 2000 is October 1995.

The mean score of the 1995 entering class was at the 59.6 percentile.

Additional Requirements and Considerations

Animal/veterinary work experience: applicants should have some veterinary medical exposure and animal work experience by November 1 of the year of application to be considered for admission. Such experience could involve breeding, rearing, feeding, and showing various species of animals including companion animals, livestock, laboratory animals, zoo animals, or wildlife. Experience in veterinary clinics and hospitals and in research laboratories is encouraged.

Recommendations from veterinarians

Extracurricular and/or community service activities

Summary of Admission Procedure

The admission procedure consists of two parts: a file review and a personal interview of applicants considered to be competitive.

Timetable

Application deadline: November 1

Notification of interview: early February

Date interviews are held: late February to early March

Date acceptances mailed: mid-March

Applicant's response date: April 15

Deposit (to hold place in class): $75.00

Deferments: are rare.

Expenses for the 1995–96 Academic Year

Tuition and fees
Resident (approximate) $ 7,600.00
Nonresident
  Contract student   To be determined
  Other nonresident $16,600.00

Living expenses (estimated) $ 4,000.00

1994–95 Admissions Summary

	Number of Applicants	Number of New Entrants
In-state	68	28
Contract	variable	3
Out-of-state	variable	5
Total:	—	36

School begins: September 25, 1995

Evaluation Criteria*

	% weight
Grades	36
Test scores	7
Animal/veterinary experience	15
Interview	24
References, personal development	11
Academic index: quality and quantity of course load, work commitments, etc.	7

* Additional points may be awarded in a "diversity/adversity" category.

UNIVERSITY OF PENNSYLVANIA

Admissions Office
School of Veterinary Medicine
University of Pennsylvania
3800 Spruce Street
Philadelphia PA 19104-6044
Telephone: (215) 898-5434

The University of Pennsylvania is located in West Philadelphia. Philadelphia is a city with a strong cultural heritage. Independence National Park includes one square mile of historic Philadelphia next to the Delaware River. Included are Independence Hall, the Liberty Bell, and many fine examples of colonial architecture. Philadelphia also offers theaters, museums, sports, and outdoor recreation. The Philadelphia Zoo, first in the nation, houses more than 1,600 mammals, birds, reptiles, and amphibians. The School of Veterinary Medicine enjoys a close relationship with the zoo.

The School of Veterinary Medicine was founded in 1884 and includes a hospital for small animals, classrooms, and research facilities in the city. The large animal hospital and research facilities are located at the New Bolton Center, a 1500-acre farm thirty-five miles west of Philadelphia. The first two years are spent on the main campus. Part of the third year may be spent at the New Bolton Center, and the fourth year is spent in rotation and electives with varying campus locations. Off-campus electives are frequently permitted.

Application Information

Applications available: July 1

Application deadline: November 1

Application fee: see VMCAS

Residency implications: priority is given to Pennsylvania residents. Contract states include New Jersey and Puerto Rico. The number of at-large places is usually 45–50, including foreign applicants.

(Veterinary Medical Colleges Application Service (VMCAS)): required for all residents and nonresidents.

Prerequisites for Admission

At least 3 English credits must be in composition; biology courses must provide background in genetics. Organic chemistry must cover aliphatic and aromatic compounds to fulfill the requirement.

Course Requirements and Semester Hours

English (including one writing course)	6
Physics, including laboratory	8
Chemistry (including at least one laboratory)	
General	8
Organic	4
Biology or zoology (3 courses)	9
Social sciences or humanities	6
Calculus	3
Electives	<u>46</u>
Total Semester Hour Credits:	90

Required undergraduate GPA: no specific GPA. Applicants are evaluated comparatively and should at least have a GPA of from 3.20 to 3.30 to be competitive. The mean cumulative GPA of the class admitted in 1994 was 3.30.

Course completion deadline: prerequisite courses must be completed by the end of the summer term of the year in which admission is sought.

Standardized examinations: Graduate Record Examination (aptitude portions only) is required. The latest acceptable test date is October of the year preceding matriculation. Scores should be received no later than December. The class admitted in 1994 had an average of 567 on the verbal subtest and 641 on the quantitative subtest.

Additional Requirements and Considerations

Animal/veterinary work experience: experience working with animals, direct veterinary work, or research experience are desired. No minimum time limit. Experience should be sufficient to convince the admissions committee of motivation, interest, and understanding.

Recommendations/evaluations: three letters of recommendation are required, one of which must come from an academic science source; the second must come from an animal/veterinary related source. The third is the choice of the applicant.

Extracurricular/community service activities: additional activities in this category can provide information important to the admissions committee.

Leadership: evidence of leadership abilities is desirable.

Summary of Admission Procedure

The University of Pennsylvania accepts about 50% of each class without interview. The remaining seats are filled through a two-part admission procedure, which includes a file review and personal interviews.

File review: files are reviewed in January by pairs of members of the admissions committee (including an alumni member), and decisions are made on whether or not to offer an interview.

Personal interviews: interviews are held on Fridays from late January until the class is filled. The number of interviews granted equals two to three times the number of seats available.

Two personal interviews are conducted: a formal interview with two faculty members (including an alumni member) of the committee, and an informal interview with student committee members. Although students do not vote on acceptance, they have a significant part in the meeting following interviews.

Timetable

Application deadline: November 1
Notification of interview: two weeks in advance of interview
Date interviews are held: Fridays from late January until completion
Date acceptances mailed: within 10 days after interview

Deposit (to hold place in class): $500.00 nonrefundable by April 15

Deferments: are considered on an individual basis.

Expenses for the 1995–96 Academic Year

Tuition and fees
Resident $20,268.00
Nonresident
   Contract student $20,268.00
   Other nonresident $24,102.00

Living expenses (estimated) $10,100–12,000 minimum

1994–95 Admissions Summary

	Number of Applicants	Number of New Entrants
In-state	160	56
Out-of-state	473	53
Total:	633	109*

* Includes four international students

School begins: September 5, 1995; orientation, August 30

Evaluation Criteria   (No percentages given)

Grades
Test scores
Animal/veterinary experience
Interview
References
Essay
English skills (TOEFL)

PURDUE UNIVERSITY   INDIANA

Denise O. Summers, Director of Student Services
School of Veterinary Medicine
1240 Lynn Hall
Purdue University
West Lafayette IN 47907-1240
Telephone: (317) 494-7893

Purdue University is located in one of the largest metropolitan centers in north-western Indiana. Greater Lafayette occupies a site on the Wabash River 65 miles northwest of Indianapolis and 126 miles southeast of Chicago. The combined population of the twin cities, Lafayette and West Lafayette, exceeds 64,000. The community offers an art museum, historical museum, 1,600 acres of public parks, and more than sixty churches of all major denominations.

Purdue ranks among the 25 largest colleges and universities in the nation. Students represent all fifty states and many foreign countries. Diversity and opportunity are goals that the School of Veterinary Medicine maintains in the selection of each year's entering class. The School of Veterinary Medicine has assumed a leading position nationally and internationally in veterinary education. To better prepare individuals for veterinary medical careers in the twenty-first century, new and innovative strategies are being considered for the curriculum, as well as teaching methods and techniques.

Application Information

Applications available: July 1

Application deadline: November 1

Application fee: See VMCAS

Residency implications: priority is given to Indiana residents. Approximately one-third of the class will be nonresident students in a total class of 60. Applicants from all states will be considered. Purdue has no contract positions. International applicants will be considered provided both the academic and financial criteria can be met.

(Veterinary Medical Colleges Application Service (VMCAS)): required for all residents and nonresidents.

Prerequisites for Admission

The course requirements outlined below are considered the bare **minimum** prerequisite courses to be completed. No less than a grade of C must be received in each required course in order to be considered eligible for admission.

In the electives category, humanities include languages, cognitive sciences, and social sciences; business writing and macroeconomics courses are highly recommended.

Concentrating electives should provide thorough preparation in an area related to the candidate's goals for the bachelor's degree program and professional career. Courses to consider in meeting the credit hour requirements include computer, basic and comparative nutrition, and general animal science courses.

Course Requirements and Semesters

English composition	2 sem.
Speech (public speaking)	1 sem.
Biology, with laboratory (diversity, development, cell structure)	2 or 3 sem.
Chemistry, general, with laboratory	2 sem.
Chemistry, organic, with laboratory **or** chemistry, organic, with laboratory (1 semester) and quantitative analysis (1 semester)	2 sem.
Biochemistry	1 or 2 sem.
Calculus	2 sem.
Physics, with laboratory	2 sem.
Genetics, with laboratory	1 sem.
Statistics	1 sem.
Electives	
Humanities	3 sem.

Required undergraduate GPA: the mean cumulative GPA of the 1994 entering class was 3.38 on a 4-point scale. The minimum overall GPA required is 2.50 on a 4.00 scale.

Course completion deadline: minimum prerequisite courses must be completed by the end of the spring term prior to matriculation.

Standardized examinations: the general tests of the GRE are required. The latest acceptable test administration is October of the year preceding matriculation in order for scores to be received on time.

Additional Requirements and Considerations

Animal/veterinary experience
Amount of college education
Recommendations/evaluations
  Academic advisor/faculty member
  Employer
  Veterinarian
Essay
Employment record
Extracurricular college experience

Summary of Admission Procedure

The admission process at Purdue University's School of Veterinary Medicine consists of:

1. A preliminary review based upon grade point indices, test scores, and prerequisite course completion
2. An in-depth review of selected applicants
3. A personal interview by invitation

Timetable

Application deadline: November 1
Notification of interview: January
Date interviews are held: February
Date acceptances mailed: March
Applicant's response date: no later than April 15

Deposit (to hold place in class): $250.00 resident; $1,000.00 nonresident.

Deferments: requests for deferments will be considered on a case-by-case basis by the Admissions Committee.

Expenses for the 1995–96 Academic Year

Tuition and fees
Resident $ 7,664.00
Nonresident
  Contract student   N/A
  Other nonresident $18,428.00

Room and board $ 4,790.00

1994–95 Admissions Summary

	Number of Applicants	Number of New Entrants
In-state	123	44
Contract	N/A	N/A
Nonresident		
Other States	377	25
International	4	0
Total:	504	69*

* Based on offers/acceptances as of 4/95. Includes two deferred applicants.

School begins: August 21, 1995

Evaluation Criteria

	% weight
Grades, test scores, overall academic performance	50
Animal, veterinary, and general work experiences, extracurricular activities, essay, overall presentation of application materials, references, and interview	50

UNIVERSITY OF TENNESSEE

College of Veterinary Medicine
University of Tennessee
P.O. Box 1071
Knoxville TN 37901-1071
Telephone: (615) 974-7263

The University of Tennessee's College of Veterinary Medicine is located in Knoxville, a city of 165,000 situated in the Appalachian foothills of East Central Tennessee. Only 45 minutes from the Great Smoky Mountains National Park and three hours from both Nashville and Atlanta, Knoxville offers recreational and cultural opportunities, including a symphony orchestra, an opera company, and several fine theaters. The climate in Knoxville is moderate with four distinct seasons.

The 417-acre Knoxville campus of the University of Tennessee has about 19,000 undergraduate and 5,300 graduate students. The modern Clyde M. York Veterinary Medicine Building, housing the teaching and research facilities, Veterinary Teaching Hospital, and Agriculture-Veterinary Medicine Library, faces the Tennessee River on the University's Agricultural Campus.

The curriculum of the College of Veterinary Medicine is a nine-semester, four-year program. Development of a strong basic science education is emphasized in the first year. The second and third years emphasize the study of diseases, their causes, diagnosis, treatment, and prevention. An innovative feature of this curriculum allows the individual student to select his or her course of study in semester six to achieve specific educational/career goals through the selection of appropriate elective courses. In the fourth year, students participate exclusively in clinical rotations in the Veterinary Teaching Hospital including unique programs in zoo and exotic animal medicine and surgery, cancer diagnosis and therapy, endoscopy, and laser surgery.

Application Information

Applications available: July 1

Application deadline: November 1

Residency implications: priority is given to Tennessee residents. Tennessee has no contractual agreements and does accept applications at large.

(Veterinary Medical Colleges Application Service (VMCAS)): required for all residents and nonresidents.

Application fee supplement: $15.00. The University of Tennessee requires a processing fee to develop and maintain each student's computerized database. **Do**

not send this fee to VMCAS. You will be contacted by the University of Tennessee, College of Veterinary Medicine, after VMCAS receives your application.

Course Requirements and Semester Hours

General inorganic chemistry with laboratory	8
Organic chemistry with laboratory	8
General biology/zoology with laboratory	8
Cellular biology	3
Genetics	3
Biochemistry, exclusive of laboratory*	4
Physics with laboratory	8
English composition	6
Social sciences/humanities	<u>18</u>
Total semester credit hours:	66

* This should be a complete upper division course in general biochemistry. Half of a two-semester sequence will *not* satisfy this requirement.

Required undergraduate GPA: for nonresident applicants, the minimum acceptable cumulative GPA is 3.2 on a 4-point scale. At time of acceptance, the mean GPA of the class entering in fall of 1995 was 3.44.

Course completion deadline: prerequisite courses must be completed by the end of the spring term prior to entry.

Standardized examinations: Veterinary College Admission Test is required. The VCAT must have been taken within 24 months of the application deadline date.

Additional Requirements and Considerations

Animal/veterinary work experience
Recommendations/evaluations
Extracurricular and/or community service activities
Leadership skills
Autobiographical essay

Summary of Admission Procedure

The University of Tennessee's admission procedure consists of an initial file review followed by an interview of selected applicants.

Timetable

Application deadline: VMCAS: November 1
Notification of interview: first week in March
Date interviews are held: March 18–22, 1996
Date acceptances mailed: no later than April 1
Applicant's response date: April 15

Deposit (to hold place in class): none required.

Deferments: are considered on a case-by-case basis.

Expenses for the 1995–96 Academic Year

Tuition and fees (per year)
Resident $4,390.00
Nonresident
  Contract student   N/A
  Other nonresident $9,840.00

Living expenses (estimated) $6,000–$8,000

1994–95 Admissions Summary

	Number of Applicants	Number of New Entrants
In-state	111	43
Contract	N/A	N/A
Out-of-state	233	19
Total:	344	62

School begins: August 23, 1995; August 21, 1996

Evaluation Criteria   (Evaluation is not percentage based)

Grades
Test scores (VCAT)
Animal/veterinary experience
Interview
References
Essay

Special Programs

Academic Program for Veterinary Students: zoo and exotic animal medicine and surgery program. Four- to six-week senior block to pursue specialized interests either at the college or as an "out-rotation."

Program for African-American High School Students: The University of Tennessee College of Veterinary Medicine is offering a new program that provides African-American high school students an opportunity to gain experience by working with a veterinarian in their home town for eight weeks during the summer. During one week of this summer experience, students will be guests of the College of Veterinary Medicine on the campus of The University of Tennessee, Knoxville.

To qualify, a student must be an African-American resident of Tennessee who is enrolled as a senior or junior in a Tennessee high school. Applicants must also have an interest in veterinary medicine as a potential career. Preference will be given to applicants who are currently high school seniors. Students will be paid $5.50 per hour for 40 hours each week.

Additional information is available from Dr. Christine Jenkins, Coordinator of Minority Affairs, The University of Tennessee, College of Veterinary Medicine, P.O. Box 1071, Knoxville TN 37901-1071.

TEXAS A & M UNIVERSITY

Office of the Dean
College of Veterinary Medicine
Texas A & M University
College Station TX 77843
Telephone: (409) 845-5051

The College of Veterinary Medicine is located adjacent to the cities of Bryan and College Station. The two cities have a combined population of about 100,000. Annual rainfall is about forty inches and daily temperature in July and August reaches nearly 100 degrees while the winters are mild.

The student population at Texas A & M is more than 40,000 and about 50 percent female. About 55 percent of veterinary students are female.

Application Information

Applications available: July 15

Application deadline: October 1

Residency implications: Texas has no contractual agreements with other states. Applicants from other states who have outstanding credentials will also be considered. Successful candidates who are able to compete for Academic Excellent Scholarships may attend at resident tuition rate.

(Veterinary Medical Colleges Application Service (VMCAS)): required for all residents and nonresidents.

Prerequisites for Admission

The minimal number of college or university credits required for admission into the professional curriculum is 64 semester hours. Applicants must have completed or have in progress approximately 48 credit hours during the semester they apply. Because there is no specific degree plan associated with preveterinary education, students are encouraged to pursue a specific degree plan that meets individual interests. Students are strongly encouraged to choose courses with the assistance of a knowledgeable counselor at the undergraduate institution or through contact with an academic advisor at the College of Veterinary Medicine, Texas A & M University [telephone: 800-874-9591].

Required Courses

There are no specific course prerequisites. The following courses or subject areas are required:

Life Sciences

General biology with laboratory   4 semester hours
   Survey of contemporary biology that covers the chemical basis of life, structure
   and biology of the cell, molecular biology, and genetics
General microbiology with laboratory   4 semester hours
   Basic microbiology; comparative morphology, taxonomy, pathogenesis, ecol-
   ogy, variation, and physiology of microorganisms
Genetics   3 semester hours
   Basic concepts of mammalian genetics
Nutrition   3 semester hours
   Emphasis on basic principles of human or animal nutrition; nutritional roles
   of carbohydrates, proteins, lipids, minerals, vitamins, and water; emphasis on
   digestion, absorption, metabolism and excretion of the nutrients and their
   metabolites

Chemical-Physical Sciences and Mathematics

Inorganic chemistry with laboratory   8 semester hours
   Basic concepts of modern inorganic chemistry
Organic chemistry with laboratory   4 semester hours
   Basic concepts of modern organic chemistry
Biochemistry   3 semester hours
   An introduction to the chemistry and metabolism of biologically important
   molecules, the biochemical basis of life processes, and cellular metabolism
   and regulation
Calculus/Statistics   3 semester hours
Physics with laboratory   8 semester hours
   Fundamentals of mechanics, heat, sound, electricity, and light

Nonscience

Composition and rhetoric   3 semester hours
Literature   3 semester hours
Speech communication   3 semester hours
Technical writing   3 semester hours

Additional credits
   In addition to the 52 credit hours recommended above, an applicant must
   complete a minimum of 12 additional credits. Applicants should keep in mind
   their degree program, the core curriculum requirements for a baccalaureate
   degree at Texas A & M University, and their personal career goals in making
   these choices. Applicants are strongly encouraged to make these choices with
   a qualified counselor at their institution.

Required undergraduate GPA: the minimal overall GPA required is 2.75 on a
4-point scale or 3.0 for the last 45 semester credits. The mean of the most recent
entering class was 3.5.

Course completion deadline: preveterinary courses must be completed by the
end of the spring term prior to entry.

Standardized examinations: the college requires a GRE score to be submitted
in support of the application. Standardized test scores must be 5 years old or

less. The class entering in 1995 averaged 1163 (combined Verbal and Quantitative subtests) on the GRE.

Additional Requirements and Considerations

Evaluations

Animal/veterinary work experience

Knowledge and experience in working with animals is crucial to becoming a successful veterinarian. While the professional curriculum is almost totally devoted to the understanding of animals, animal contact, experience, and handling should also be a major consideration in the preveterinary training period. Applicants are expected to be familiar with animal systems and behavior. For those interested in farm animal veterinary medicine, general agriculture knowledge should also be a major consideration. To obtain this experience, applicants should either register for course work based on their background, interests, and needs, or involve themselves in practical animal operations in the private sector. If designated courses in the animal sciences are not available at the applicant's institution, demonstrable experience with animals is acceptable. Formal training in animal systems and animal behavior is highly desirable and encouraged if available at the applicant's institution.

Summary of Admission Procedure

Texas A & M has a two-part admission procedure: applications are accepted and qualified applicants are interviewed.

Timetable

Application deadline: October 1
Notification of interview: approximately December 1
Date interviews are held: before January 15
Date acceptances mailed: approximately March 15
Applicant's response date: April 15

Deposit (to hold place in class): none required.

Deferments: the College of Veterinary Medicine at Texas A & M University limits delayed admission to the provisions of the Policy on Delayed Admission, handled on a case-by-case basis and approved by the Associate Dean for Academic Programs.

Expenses for the 1995–96 Academic Year

Tuition and fees (for first-year students)

Resident	$ 5,400.00
Nonresident	
Contract student	N/A
Other nonresident	$16,200.00
Books and supplies	$ 1,645.00
Living expenses (approximate)	
Room and board	$ 4,000.00
Personal	$ 3,000.00

1994–95 Admissions Summary

	Number of Applicants	Number of New Entrants
In-state	401	120
Contract	N/A	N/A
Out-of-state	114	8
Total:	515	128

School begins: late August of each academic year

Evaluation Criteria   (No percentages given)

Academic performance
MCAT or GRE score
Interview
Essay
Personal evaluations (three evaluations are required)
Semester course load

The Selections Committee evaluates, individually and collectively, the complete application portfolio of each applicant. All components of the portfolio are evaluated subjectively.

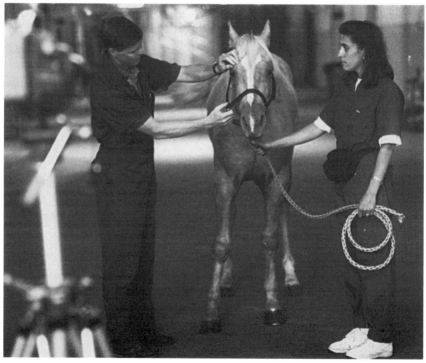

A visiting senior student from an international veterinary school and a large animal clinician evaluate this equine patient who is exhibiting signs of tetanus at the Purdue University Veterinary Medical Teaching Hospital.

TUFTS UNIVERSITY   MASSACHUSETTS

Office of Admissions
School of Veterinary Medicine
Tufts University
200 Westborough Road
North Grafton MA 01536
Telephone: (508) 839-7920

Tufts University is located on both an urban and a rural campus in and near Boston where sports and cultural activities abound. The School of Veterinary Medicine provides an exciting biomedical environment for the study of modern veterinary medicine. Signature programs include wildlife medicine, equine sports medicine, international veterinary medicine, biotechnology and veterinary medicine, and the study of issues related to ethical dimensions of veterinary medicine, including animal welfare.

Hands-on learning begins in the first year during a course on clinical skills and animal behavior and continues throughout the next three years. Many opportunities exist outside of formal courses for hands-on work in hospitals and research laboratories. The Hospital for Large Animals, Foster Hospital for Small Animals, the Ambulatory Clinic, and the Wildlife Clinic see more than 13,000 cases annually, providing a rich mixture of horses, cats, dogs, cattle, sheep, goats, and native wildlife.

Application Information

Applications available: July

Application deadline: January 1

Application fee: $60.00

Residency implications: Massachusetts residents make up about half of each class. All others considered for the remaining spaces. Tufts' contracts include: Rhode Island 4, New Hampshire 1, and New Mexico 1.

(Veterinary Medical Colleges Application Service (VMCAS)): no participation.

Prerequisites for Admission

Course and Semester Requirements

Biology, with laboratory	2 sem.
Inorganic chemistry, with laboratory	2 sem.
Organic chemistry, with laboratory	2 sem.
Physics	2 sem.

Mathematics	2 sem.
Genetics, unless included in biology	1 sem.
Biochemistry	1 sem.
English composition	2 sem.
Social and behavioral sciences	2 sem.
Humanities and fine arts	2 sem.

Required undergraduate GPA: no minimum GPA required. The average GPA for the class admitted in 1995 is 3.26.

Course completion deadline: prerequisite courses must be completed by time of matriculation into the D.V.M. program.

Standardized examinations: Graduate Record Examination (general test only) is required. The latest acceptable test date for applicants to the Class of 2000 is December 1995. GRE scores are valid for five years; the exam must have been taken during or after 1990. Average GRE scores for the Class of 1999 were: verbal 590, quantitative 640, analytical 690.

Additional Requirements and Considerations

Animal/veterinary/biomedical research experience
Recommendations/evaluations
Essays
Interview

Summary of Admission Procedure

Tufts' admission procedure consists of a review of the application and an interview of selected applicants.

Timetable

Application deadline: January 1
Notification of interview: end of January
Date interviews are held: February
Date acceptances mailed: March/April
Applicant's response date: April 15

Deposit (to hold place in class): $500.00

Deferments: requests for deferment are handled on a case-by-case basis.

Expenses for the 1995–96 Academic Year

Tuition and fees
Contract student	$ 5,496–12,496
Out-of-state resident	$24,496.00
Massachusetts resident	$22,096.00

Living expenses (estimated)
| Single | $ 8,250.00 |

1994–95 Admissions Summary

	Number of Applicants	Number of New Entrants
Total:	675	75

School begins: August 28, 1995

Special Academic Programs for Veterinary Students

Equine Sports Medicine: the Equisport program brings students into close contact with performance horses. Veterinary personnel and state-of-the-art equipment are at work 24 hours each day to fulfill the training, rehabilitative, and diagnostic needs of their equine clients.

Wildlife Medicine: emphasizes the importance of all creatures, their interrelationship, and the significance of comparative medicine.

Biotechnology: in cooperation with leading biomedical research institutions in Massachusetts, faculty and students hope to produce animals with better natural disease resistance, a supply of valuable medical compounds, and animal products with less fat.

International Veterinary Medicine: an interdisciplinary program in third world development is offered, with the realization that veterinarians will play an increasingly important role in offering expertise and experience to resolve global food and disease problems.

Ethics and Values in Veterinary Medicine: issues of animal welfare and the complicated ethical problems surrounding them are addressed in a highly developed veterinary ethics program.

TUSKEGEE UNIVERSITY

ALABAMA

Tuskegee University
School of Veterinary Medicine
Tuskegee AL 36088
Telephone: (205) 727-8460

Tuskegee University School of Veterinary Medicine is located in Tuskegee, Alabama, a city of about 25,000. Tuskegee is located about forty miles east of Montgomery and forty miles west of Columbus, Georgia. Summers are hot and humid and winters are moderate. Numerous lakes, parks, recreational facilities, and other educational institutions are located nearby.

The university was founded by Booker T. Washington in 1845, and the veterinary school was established in 1945. Seventy percent of black veterinarians in the United States received their professional training at Tuskegee. A large portion of the campus has been declared a historical site by the National Park Service.

Application Information

Applications available: July 1

Application deadline: December 7

Application fee: $25.00

Residency implications: applications are accepted nationwide, with 14 spaces under contract as follows: Arkansas 2, Georgia 2, Kentucky 2, New Jersey 2, South Carolina 4, West Virginia 1, and Puerto Rico 1, leaving 46 spaces at large.

Prerequisites for Admission

In the physical sciences, the courses in organic chemistry and physics, including laboratory, should cover one academic year.

Minimum Acceptable Admission Requirements and Semester Credit Hours

English composition/communications	6 hours
Mathematics (algebra and trigonometry)	6 hours
Chemistry (minimum)	
General chemistry (with laboratory)	8 hours
Organic chemistry (with laboratory)	4 hours
Biochemistry (with laboratory)	4 hours
*Physics (includes laboratory)	8 hours
Biological science	

112

Basic biology (with laboratory)	8 hours
**Advanced biology	9 hours
Free electives	8 hours
(advanced biological science—optional)	
Animal science	9 hours
(includes poultry and animal nutrition)	
Social science and humanities	6 hours
(electives)	

* One academic year

** Advanced biology courses, e.g., zoology, microbiology, genetics, anatomy, physiology, and histology

Required undergraduate GPA: the requirement is 2.70 on a 4-point scale.

Course completion deadline: prerequisite courses must be completed by the end of the spring semester of the year of application.

Standardized examinations: Veterinary College Admission Test (VCAT), which must be taken within five years of application, is required.

Summary of Admission Procedure

The following items are taken into consideration: academic record, academic trends, letters of recommendation, work experience, and VCAT scores.

Timetable

Application deadline: December 7
Notification of interview: February
Date interviews are held: February–March
Date acceptances mailed: April 1
Applicant's response date: May 30

Deposit (to hold place in class): $275.00

Deferments: are not offered; applicant may request folder be activated for next year.

Expenses for the 1993–94 Academic Year

(No data received for 1994-95 or 1995-96)

All Alabama residents and SREB contract students receive a $500.00 per year voucher to offset their tuition.

Tuition and fees	*Year 1 & 2* *Students*	*Year 3 & 4* *Students*
Residents	$ 8,170.00	$ 8,170.00
Nonresidents	$ 8,170.00	$ 8,170.00
Living expenses (estimated)	$ 5,000.00	$ 7,000.00
Total:	$13,170.00	$15,170.00

1994–95 Admissions Summary

	Number of Applicants	Number of New Entrants
In-state	18	8
Contract	75	16
Out-of-state	<u>135</u>	<u>37</u>
Total:	228	61

School begins: late August

Evaluation Criteria

	% weight
Grades	50
Test scores	5
Animal/veterinary experience	10
Interview	25
References	5
Essay	5

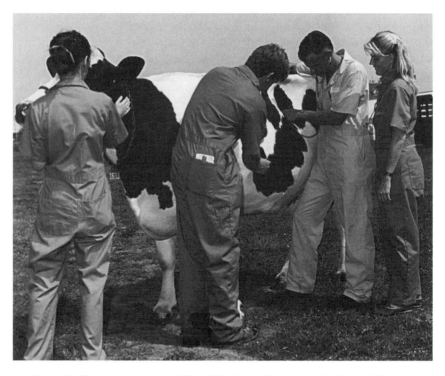

Dr. Bruce Hull, a veterinarian at The Ohio State University College of Veterinary Medicine, is shown with senior veterinary students while demonstrating a technique for listening to a cow's abdomen.

PHOTO BY JOHN J. SWARTZ

Virginia Polytechnic Institute and State University

Virginia-Maryland Regional College of Veterinary Medicine
Virginia Polytechnic Institute and State University
Blacksburg VA 24061-0443
Telephone: (703) 231-4699

The Virginia-Maryland Regional College of Veterinary Medicine is situated on three distinct campuses. The main campus is at Virginia Tech in Blacksburg, Virginia, a community with a population of about 40,000 situated on a high plateau in southwestern Virginia between the Blue Ridge and Allegheny mountain ranges. Its residents enjoy a wide range of educational, social, recreational, and cultural opportunities. In addition to the Blacksburg campus, the Equine Medical Center campus is in Leesburg, Virginia, and the University of Maryland is at College Park. The college received full accreditation in 1994 from the American Veterinary Medical Association.

In recognition of a need for veterinarians trained in both basic and clinical sciences, the college offers students the opportunity to participate in graduate studies and receive appropriate advanced training to conduct research in basic or clinical disciplines. Nearly 25 percent of the nation's veterinarians work in areas other than private practice, such as government and corporate veterinary medicine. Through the assistance of a grant from the Pew Charitable Trusts, the college has established a Center for Government and Corporate Veterinary Medicine, which is a national resource for training veterinarians for the wide variety of careers in this area of the profession.

Application Information

Applications available: September 1

Application deadline: November 15

Application fee: $45.00

Application availability: Virginia residents and nonresidents contact (703) 231-4699. Maryland residents contact (301) 935-6083, extension 116.

Residency implications: Maryland or Virginia resident status required.

(Veterinary Medical Colleges Application Service (VMCAS)): required for all nonresidents.

Prerequisites for Admission

Course Requirements and Semester Hours

Biological sciences, with laboratories	8
Organic chemistry, with laboratories	8
Physics, with laboratories	8
Biochemistry, without laboratory	3
English (composition, 3 credit hours)	6
Humanities/social science	6
Mathematics	6

Students must earn a *C* or better in all required courses.

Required undergraduate GPA: to be considered for admission, applicants must have a cumulative undergraduate GPA of at least 2.8 on a 4-point scale upon completion of a minimum of two academic years of full-time study (60 semester/ 90 quarter hours) at an accredited college or university. Alternatively, a 3.3 GPA in the last two years (60 semester hours) will qualify a student who does not have a 2.8 GPA overall. All courses taken during this two-year period must be junior or senior level. The mean GPA of those accepted into the Class of 1999 was 3.37.

Course completion deadline: required courses must be completed by the end of the spring term of the year in which matriculation occurs.

Standardized examinations: Graduate Record Examination, aptitude and advanced biology sections, is required. For the Class of 1999, the mean score on the aptitude portion (verbal, quantitative, analytical) was 1850, and the mean score for the advanced biology portion was in the 61st percentile. The oldest acceptable scores must be within five years of the application deadline.

Additional Requirements and Considerations

Maturity and a broad cultural perspective
Motivation and dedication to a career in veterinary medicine
Evidence of potential, and appreciation of the career opportunities for veterinarians, as indicated by achievements in the following areas:
    Nonveterinary work, veterinary and animal related work, research, industrial, government and corporate practice, and other biomedically related experience
    Extramural activities
    Achievements, awards, and other recognitions

Summary of Admission Procedure

The Virginia-Maryland Regional College of Veterinary Medicine has a three-part admission procedure, comprising an initial screening of applicants by the Admissions and Standards Committee with input from the college faculty, an interview of selected applicants, and a final review of the dossiers of all interviewees by the Admissions and Standards Committee.

Timetable

Application deadline: November 15
Notification of interview: usually during the third week in January

Date interviews are held: mid- to late February
Date acceptances mailed: early March
Applicant's response date: April 15

Deposit (to hold place in class): $400.00

Deferments: case-by-case basis if a candidate has extenuating circumstances beyond his or her control.

Expenses for the 1995–96 Academic Year

Tuition and fees

Resident	$ 8,207.00
Nonresident	
Contract student	N/A
Other nonresident	$19,500.00

Living expenses (estimated)

For each of first three years	$10,000.00
For the fourth year	$14,000.00

1994–95 Admissions Summary

	Number of Applicants	Number of New Entrants
In-state		
Maryland	97	30
Virginia	151	50
Contract	N/A	N/A
Out-of-state	N/A	N/A
Total:	248	80

School begins: August 21, 1995

Evaluation Criteria

	% weight
Academics	50
Cumulative GPA, required science GPA, last 60 semester hour GPA, GRE Aptitude, GRE Biology	
Background	25
Related animal experience; veterinary experience; research, industrial, and commercial experience; activities, achievements, and awards; narrative and personal references	
Interviews	25

Special Academic Programs for Veterinary Students

The college has established the Center for Government and Corporate Veterinary Medicine to provide specialized training in the senior year to veterinary students interested in careers outside private clinical practice. Examples of opportunities include Zoo and Wildlife Medicine, Aquatic and Marine Mammals, Epidemiology, Regulatory, Pathology, Toxicology, Lab Animals, or Avian.

The competitive applicant at the college in recent years has had a cumulative GPA of 3.4, GRE general score of 1850, GRE Biology subject test of the 60th percentile, a wide variety of animal experience— —both large and small, worked for a veterinarian for 400-600 hours, and worked in a research laboratory or been involved in commercial or industrial settings related to veterinary medicine. If you possess these qualifications, you are encouraged to submit your application.

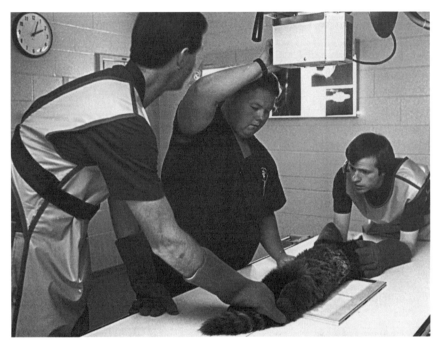

Staff veterinarians, both graduates of The Ohio State University College of Veterinary Medicine, are shown with a veterinary technician preparing for a lateral x-ray of a raccoon at the Columbus Zoo.

PHOTO BY JOHN J. SWARTZ

WASHINGTON STATE UNIVERSITY

Office of Student Services
College of Veterinary Medicine
Washington State University
Pullman WA 99164-7012
Telephone: (509) 335-1532

Washington State University, enrollment 17,000, is located in southeastern Washington in the town of Pullman. This small community is surrounded by farmland yet is close to the mountains of Idaho. The area offers good summer and winter recreation.

The College of Veterinary Medicine at WSU was founded in 1899 and is one of the five oldest Colleges of Veterinary Medicine in the country. Washington, Oregon, and Idaho (WOI) have developed a regional program in veterinary medical education that also serves Alaska, Arizona, Hawaii, Montana, Nevada, New Mexico, North Dakota, Utah, and Wyoming through the Western Interstate Commission for Higher Education (WICHE) Compact.

The D.V.M. degree is awarded by Washington State University and Oregon State University. The University of Idaho is a full partner in the program, but Idaho students receive their D.V.M. degrees from Washington.

Application Information

Applications available: August 1

Application deadline: November 1

Application fee: see VMCAS

Residency implications: priority is given to Washington and Idaho residents. WOI contracts include WICHE states (Alaska, Arizona, Hawaii, Montana, Nevada, North Dakota, New Mexico, Utah, Wyoming) with 16 places. Washington accepts a few nonresidents each year from states other than contracts listed above.

(Veterinary Medical Colleges Application Service (VMCAS)): required for all residents and nonresidents.

Prerequisites for Admission

Total minimum number of credits required is 60 semester hours or 90 quarter hours.

Course Requirements	Required Hours
Chemistry	A sequence of inorganic and organic courses with laboratories and one upper-division biochemistry course

119

Mathematics	Sufficient to meet the prerequisites for inorganic chemistry and physics
Physics	One semester or one quarter of college level physics for science majors
Zoology or biology	One-year sequence
Genetics	One semester or quarter

Recommended undergraduate GPA: a minimum overall GPA of 3.20 (or 3.30 for the last 45 semester credit hours) on a 4-point scale is recommended. The Class of 1999 had a mean overall GPA of 3.50 at the time of acceptance.

Course completion deadline: prerequisite courses must be completed by June 15 prior to entry.

Standardized examinations: Graduate Record Examination (General Test) is required. The latest acceptable test date for applicants to the Class of 2000 is December 1995. The mean combined score on the *Graduate Record Examination* for the Class of 1998 was at the 62nd percentile.

Additional Requirements and Considerations

Animal/veterinary work experience
Recommendations from veterinarians
Extracurricular and/or community service activities

Summary of Admission Procedure

The Washington-Oregon-Idaho admission procedure consists of two parts, a file review and a personal interview of applicants considered to be competitive.

Timetable

Application deadline: November 1
Notification of interview: February
Date interviews are held: mid-February to late March
Date acceptances mailed: before March 15 (WA, OR, ID, and at large); before April 1 (WICHE)
Applicants response date: two weeks (WA, OR, ID); as soon as possible, but no later than April 15 (WICHE); as soon as possible, but no later than April 15 (at large)

Deposit (to hold place in class): $50.00

Deferments: are considered for financial reasons and completion of graduate degrees.

Expenses for the 1994–95 Academic Year

Tuition and fees	
Resident	$ 7,458.00
Nonresident	
Contract student	$ 7,458.00
Other nonresidents	$18,934.00
Living expenses (estimated)	$3,200–$4,000

1994–95 Admissions Summary

	Number of Applicants	Number of New Entrants
Washington	169	42
Idaho	45	11
Contract	174	6
Out-of-state	260	3
Total:	648	62

* Note: see also section under Oregon State University; Oregon residents apply to Oregon State University.

School begins: August 29, 1995

Evaluation Criteria**

	% weight
Grades	37
Test scores	8
Animal/veterinary experience	15
Interview	22
References	11
Academic index (consideration of entire academic record)	7

** Diversity is considered in several criteria.

Special Programs

D.V.M.-Research Track: since the fall of 1989, eight students in entering classes have been selected. In addition to completing the regular D.V.M. curriculum, students in the research track are assigned additional tasks designed to develop them for research careers. A limited number of stipends are available for students in this program.

UNIVERSITY OF WISCONSIN

Office of Academic Affairs
School of Veterinary Medicine
University of Wisconsin-Madison
2015 Linden Drive West
Madison WI 53706
Telephone: (608) 263-2525

The University of Wisconsin is located in Madison, the state capital, which has a population of about 190,000. Consistently ranked among the nation's "most livable" cities, its hilly terrain, scattered parks and woodlands saturate the urban setting with a friendly neighborhood atmosphere. Centered on a narrow isthmus among four scenic lakes, the city is a recreational paradise. The University sprawls over nine hundred acres along Lake Mendota and its population is nearly 45,000. It has rated among the top ten universities academically since 1910 and is third in the country in volume of research activity.

The School of Veterinary Medicine facility has a modern veterinary teaching hospital, modern equipment and high quality lab space for teaching, research, and classrooms. The curriculum provides a broad education in veterinary medicine with learning experiences in food animal medicine and other specialty areas. The school also pioneered a unique Senior Rotation in Ambulatory Service for fourth-year students where they experience the life and work of a veterinarian specializing in large animal medicine by working in one of twenty practices near Madison. The school has an outstanding research program with faculty in the forefront. Many faculty members have joint appointments with the College of Agriculture, Medical School, Regional Primate Center, McArdle Cancer Research Institute, the National Wildlife Health Laboratory, and the North Central Dairy Forage Center. These outside links provide research and job opportunities for students.

Application Information

Applications available: July

Application deadline: November 15

Application fee supplement: $35.00

Wisconsin has a cooperative agreement with the Pontifical Catholic University of Puerto Rico to annually offer admission to up to two students from the Pontifical Catholic University of Puerto Rico. Students from Puerto Rico considering applying to the BS/DVM Binary Program should contact the College of Sciences, Pontifical Catholic University of Puerto Rico, Estacion 6, Ponce, Puerto Rico 00732.

Residency implications: between 60 and 70 Wisconsin residents will be accepted. Wisconsin has no contractual agreements, but may accept 10–20 nonresidents.

(Veterinary Medical Colleges Application Service (VMCAS)): required for all nonresidents.

Prerequisites for Admission

Applicants must complete a minimum of 60 semester credits of college course work. The 60 credits include the required 40–43 credits of course work listed below, plus a minimum of 17 credits of elective course work left to the student's discretion. The 17 elective credits allow the student to meet personal and academic goals and objectives while preparing for admission to veterinary school. All course work must be completed no later than the end of the spring term prior to admission to the program.

Course Requirements and Semester Hours

Biochemistry, organic chemistry must be prerequisite　3
General biology **or** zoology, introductory animal biology course　5
　with laboratory
General **and** qualitative chemistry, two-semester lecture series　8
　with laboratory
Organic chemistry, one-semester lecture satisfying biochemistry　3
　prerequisite
English composition **or** journalism　3–6
　(must include completion of **either** of the following):
　1. satisfactory score on a college English placement exam, **or**
　2. an introductory English composition course, **plus**
　　　completion of one of the following:
　　a. an English composition or journalism course graded on
　　　　the basis of writing skills, **or,**
　　b. written evidence from instructor that writing skills
　　　　were included in the grading of a specific college-
　　　　level course
Genetics **or** animal breeding, must include principles of　3
　heredity and preferably molecular mechanisms
General physics, two-semester lecture series　6
Statistics, introductory course　3
Social science/humanities, any elective courses in social science　6
　or the humanities

Total Semester Hours Credits:　40–43

Required undergraduate GPA: not stipulated. The mean cumulative GPA of the Class of 1999 is approximately 3.53 for residents and 3.76 for nonresidents.

Course completion deadline: all course work must be completed no later than the spring 1996 term prior to admission in the fall 1996 term.

Standardized examinations: Graduate Record Examination, General Aptitude subtest, is required. The GRE may be taken no later than October in the year of application. The mean score of the Class of 1998 for the verbal, quantitative, and analytical portions combined is approximately 1835 for residents and 2030 for nonresidents.

Additional Considerations

Animal contact and work experience
Veterinary medical experience
Other preparatory experience
College degrees earned
Extracurricular activities
Letters of reference

Summary of Admission Procedure

The University of Wisconsin has a two-part admission procedure:

1. *Evaluation of academic record*
   Undergraduate cumulative GPA
   Required course GPA
   Most recent 30-semester credit GPA
   Graduate Record Examination score
2. *Evaluation of personal experience and characteristics*
   Animal and veterinary work experience
   Other preparatory experience (includes extracurricular activities)
   Personal history/academic performance (summary category to include review of academic history, academic achievements, diversity of background, etc.)
   Reference letters

Timetable

Application deadline: November 15
Interviews: none
Date acceptances mailed: early March
Applicant's response date: April 15

Deposit (to hold place in class): none required

Deferments: are considered on an individual basis by the admissions committee and may be granted for extenuating circumstances.

Expenses for the 1995–96 Academic Year

The exact tuition-fee schedule is determined annually. Living expenses include room and board, books and supplies, microscope needed the first year, and miscellaneous other expenses.

Tuition and fees (estimated)	
Resident	$ 8,892.00
Nonresident	
Contract student	N/A
Other nonresident	$12,840.00
Living expenses (estimated)	$ 7,300.00
Books and supplies	$ 940.00

1994–95 Admissions Summary

	Number of Applicants	Number of New Entrants
In-state	178	70
Contract	N/A	N/A
Out-of-state	416	10
Total:	594	80

School begins: September 1, 1995

Evaluation Criteria

Each year the Admissions Committee determines the selection criteria for admission. For the fall 1994 admission year, the class was selected based upon the following comparative evaluation:

1. The academic preparation of the applicants (weighted approximately 60 percent)
2. The personal background and experience of the applicants (weighted approximately 40 percent)

Special Admissions Program

Early Notification of Admission: Wisconsin resident applicants who have exceptional qualifications for admission may receive a letter of offer early in the selection process. Notification of early acceptance would be no later than February 26 with an applicant's response date of April 15, 1996.

Special Academic Programs for Veterinary Students

Production Medicine Series: problem-based approach to learning production medicine, including computerized production analysis, nutrition, and mastitis control/treatment.

International Veterinary Medicine: arrangement with Costa Rica for a food animal experience supervised by the Veterinary Medical School in Bogota.

UNIVERSITY OF GUELPH

ONTARIO

Admissions, Office of the Registrar
University of Guelph
Guelph Ontario N1G 2W1
Canada
Telephone (519) 824-4120, Ext. 6062
or
Assistant Dean
Ontario Veterinary College
Telephone: (519) 824-4120, Ext. 4413

Founded in 1862, the Ontario Veterinary College is located in Guelph about sixty miles north of Buffalo. Guelph has a similar climate to Detroit and Chicago. Surrounded by gently rolling farmland, this city of 90,000 is typical of the Northeast.

The university has an enrollment of 14,000 undergraduate students, of whom 400 are veterinary students. There are also 150 graduate students, 120 faculty and 200 staff at the veterinary college, which offers degree programs leading to a D.V.M., M.Sc., Ph.D., Doctor of Veterinary Science (D.V.Sc.) and a Graduate Diploma. The college has five departments, including Population Medicine, Clinical Studies, Biomedical Sciences, Veterinary Microbiology and Immunology, Pathology, and a full service teaching hospital. Funding for research comes from a $6 million research grant base. There is also a large, modern research station for separately housing sheep, swine, and dairy and beef cattle.

Application Information

Applications available: October 1

Application deadline: February 1

Application fee: $75.00

Residency implications for applicants: applications will be considered from Canadian citizens, those with permanent resident status in Canada, and students from a country without a veterinary college. The applicant must have lived in the Province of Ontario for one year, not in attendance at a post-secondary institution.

(Veterinary Medical Colleges Application Service (VMCAS)): no participation.

Prerequisites for Admission

Applicants are selected for admission only to the preveterinary year. This is the only entry to the D.V.M. program.

126

Course Requirements

Biology	2 semester courses
Chemistry or "chemistry-related" courses	2 semester courses
Physics	1 semester course
Mathematics: calculus or a statistics course with a calculus prerequisite	1 semester course
Humanities (philosophy preferred) and/or social science	2 semester courses
Electives	2 semester courses

Required undergraduate GPA: students with a minimum A (80.0) based on the average of the required courses and the last 2 semesters in full-time attendance at university may be invited to interview. The average grade of the class recently admitted to the preveterinary year was 85.0.

Course completion deadline: required courses must be completed by June 15 of the year of application in order to receive an invitation to interview.

Standardized examinations: none required.

Additional Considerations

Reasons for choosing a career in veterinary medicine
Quality of preparatory academic program
Experience and knowledge in matters relating to animals and to the veterinary medical profession
Experience and achievement in extracurricular affairs and/or community service activities
Personal characteristics
Communication skills

Summary of Admission Procedure

The two-part admission procedure includes a review of academic achievement and a personal interview by invitation only.

Timetable

Application deadline: February 1
Notification of interview: begins May 15
Date interviews are held: June 15–30
Date acceptances mailed: begins July 15
Applicant's response date: two weeks

Deposit (to hold place in class): none required

Deferments: up to three years are considered to complete B.Sc., M.Sc., etc., or to pursue worthy and/or veterinary related experiences.

Expenses for the 1995–96 Academic Year

The yearly totals shown are for two semesters; the amounts are given in Canadian dollars.

Tuition and fees

Resident	$ 3,000.00
Visa student	$14,000.00

Living expenses (estimated) $10,000.00

1994 Admissions Summary

Number of applicants	600
Number of new entrants	100

School begins: September 5, 1995

Evaluation Criteria

	% weight
Grades	75
Interview	25

UNIVERSITÉ DE MONTRÉAL

QUÉBEC

Service des Admissions
Université de Montréal
C.P. 6205, Succursale A
Montréal Québec H3C 3T5
Canada
Téléphone: (514) 343-2223, Attn: Mr. Claude Fagnan

Renseignements pour les applications
Application Information

Formulaires disponibles dès le: 1er décembre
Applications available: December 1

Date limite de remise: 1er mars
Application deadline: March 1

Frais d'application: 55.00 C$
Application fee: $55.00 Canadian

Statut de résident: Il faut être citoyen Canadien ou résident permanent pour être admissible. Les résidents du Québec ont généralement priorité, quoique des francophones d'autre provinces peuvent aussi être admis.
Residency implications: Canadian citizenship or permanent residency in Canada is required. Quebec residents are heavily favored, although some French speaking residents of other provinces may be admitted.

Prérequis
Prerequisites for Admission

D.E.C. (Diplôme d'Etudes Collégiales) en sciences.
D.E.C. (Collegiate Studies Diploma; obtained in Quebec) majoring in science. (The D.E.C. represents two years of post-high school studies.)

Cours
Course Requirements

Physique/*Physics*	101, 201, 301–78
Chimie/*Chemistry*	101, 201, 202
Biologie/*Biology*	301, 401
Mathématiques (avec calcul intégral)/	103, 203
Mathematics (including calculus)	

Pour être admis au programme de D.M.V., il faut: a) avoir satisfait les conditions ci-dessus, ou, b) faire preuve d'études équivalentes, ou, c) avoir atteint l'âge de 21 ans et posséder des connaissances et une expérience valables dans le programme choisi, tel qu'évaluées par le doyen.

To be considered for admission, one must: a) have completed the above requirements, or, b) have completed equivalent studies, or, c) be 21 years or older and both familiar with and experienced in the program of choice (within the D.V.M. program), as evaluated by the dean.

La maîtrise de la langue française est une condition de diplômation. Par conséquent, tout nouvel étudiant doit réussir le test de français du Ministère de l'Enseignement Supérieur et de la Science ou, s'il échoue au test, réussir les cours de français prescrits par l'Université.

Language requirements: All students entering undergraduate degree programs must show that they have mastered French in order to qualify for the degree. This graduation requirement may be met either by passing the Quebec Ministry of Education French test or by passing designated remedial French courses.

COTE Z: L'université de Montréal se sert de ce système pour comparer les dossiers académiques des étudiants. La COTE Z est calculée à partir du dossier académique. Elle représente la valeur d'un dossier dans un système d'unité commun à tous les postulants.

Requirements (GPA): The University of Montreal uses a statistical system called "COTE Z" to compare its applicants to one another. The COTE Z is based on the applicant's academic record and calculates its value in a unit system common to all applicants.

Complétion des cours: Le candidat doit, ou bien avoir terminé, ou s'être inscrit à tous les cours prérequis au moment de l'application.

Course completion deadline: The applicant must be registered for or have completed all prerequisites at the time of application.

Tests d'Admission: Seul les examens de l'Université sont utilisés. Les candidats dont le dossier académique est jugé comme acceptable seront convoqués pour passer ces tests.

Standardized examinations: GRE, VCAT, and MCAT are not recognized. Applicants whose academic record is considered acceptable are given a time and place at which to take the University's own admission test. This test requires a good knowledge of French. If an applicant is not proficient in French, a remedial language course may be required.

Test de Français: Le succès à ce test n'est pas obligatoire pour l'admission mais l'étudiant doit réussir pour obtenir son diplôme.

French test: Success in passing this language test is not a prerequisite for admission to the first year of the veterinary program, but each student must pass the test successfully to earn a diploma.

Critères de sélection (priorité d'importance)
Additional Considerations (in order of importance)

1. Dossier académique
2. Tests d'admission et entrevue: l'entrevue a été structurée pour évaluer la motivation, la préparation et le raisonnement des candidats.

1. *Academic record*
2. *Admissions exam and interview: the interview is designed to verify the applicant's motivation and preparation, etc. The above list reflects priorities (applicants are judged first on academic merit, then test/exam results, etc.).*

Cédule du processus
Summary of Admission Procedure

Formulaires d'application disponible: le 1er décembre
Date limite de remise des formules: le 1er mars
Tests d'admission: mois d'avril
Entrevues: mi-mai
Notification d'acceptation/rejet des candidats: fin mai, début juin

Timetable

Applications available: December 1
Application deadline: March 1
Admissions exams (selected applicants): weekends in April
Interviews (further-selected applicants): mid-May
Notification of acceptance/refusal: end of May, early June

Dépôt nécessaire pour garder une place dans la classe: aucun
Deposit (to hold place in class): none required

L'acceptation ne peut, en aucun cas, être reportée à une année suivante.
Deferments: not considered

Budget estimatif
Estimated Expenses for the 1994–95 Academic Year

Frais de scolarité: 2,078.00 C\$
Livres, fournitures scolaires: 1,200-1,400.00 C\$
Logement et nourriture: 6,000.00 C\$
Autres dépenses: 2,500.00 C\$

Budget

Tuition and fees: 2,078.00 C\$ (1,039.00 C\$ per semester)*
Books and supplies: 1,200-1,400.00 C\$
Living expenses:
  Room and board: 6,000.00 C\$
  Personal expense: 2,500.00 C\$

* Estimated expenses are given in Canadian dollars (1 C\$ = 0.70 US\$)

Début de l'année scolaire 1994-95: 25 août 1994
Fall semester begins: August 25, 1994

Critères d'évaluation	%	Evaluation Criteria
Resultáts scolaires	50	Grades
Test d'aptitudes	20	Test scores
Entrevue	30	Interview

University of Prince Edward Island

PRINCE EDWARD ISLAND

Registrar's Office
Atlantic Veterinary College
University of Prince Edward Island
550 University Avenue
Charlottetown PEI C1A-4P3
Canada
Telephone: (902) 566-0608

Atlantic Veterinary College (AVC), the newest college of veterinary medicine in North America, was completed in 1987 and is fully accredited by the American Veterinary Medical Association. Located in Charlottetown, the capital of Prince Edward Island, the community enjoys a country lifestyle in a city that offers many of the amenities of larger cities. Residents attend presentations by the art and theatre communities as well as enjoy outdoor activities such as cycling, golfing, running, sailing, and cross-country skiing.

The college is a completely integrated teaching, research and service facility. The four-story building contains the veterinary teaching hospital, diagnostic services, fish health unit, ambulatory services, post-mortem services, animal barns, laboratories, classrooms, computer facilities, audio-visual services, research laboratories, offices, cafeteria, and study areas. The AVC also maintains a nearby farm facility.

Prince Edward Island is a scenic province with a wide variety of dairy, beef, sheep, horse, poultry, and fish farms. The combination and variety of animal and fish farms have allowed the AVC to develop special expertise in aquaculture and population medicine. The fish health unit of the AVC is the largest and most advanced aquatic species research facility of any veterinary college in North America.

Application Information

Applications available: September

Application deadline: December 1, Canadian students; April 1, international students

Application fee: $35.00 (Canadian)

Residency implications: Atlantic Veterinary College currently has contracts with: Nova Scotia (16), New Brunswick (13), Newfoundland (2), and the home province P.E.I. (10). International students are admitted on a noncontract basis (9) and Canadian residents of other provinces may also be admitted (2).

(Veterinary Medical Colleges Application Service (VMCAS)): no participation.

Prerequisites for Admission

The preveterinary program leading to admission at the Atlantic Veterinary College will normally take two years to complete.

Course Requirements

The equivalent of twenty (20) one-semester courses are required, including:
Mathematics, 2 courses including statistics
Biology, 4 courses including genetics and microbiology
Chemistry, 3 courses including organic chemistry
Physics, 1 course
English, 2 courses including one with emphasis on writing
Humanities and social sciences, 3 courses
Electives, 5 courses from any discipline
(Science courses will normally have a laboratory component.)

Required undergraduate GPA: no minimum stated; mean cumulative GPA of most recent entering class is 3.3 on a 4-point scale.

Course completion deadline: June 1 of the year of application

Standardized examinations: none required

Additional Requirements and Considerations

Veterinary related experience: at least 40 hours in large animal practice and 40 hours in small animal practice
Veterinary evaluations
Maturity and reliability
Knowledge of and interest in animals and the veterinary medical profession

Summary of Admission Procedure

Academic credentials and animal work experience are objectively evaluated by the Registrar's Office. Personal characteristics, leadership ability, and extracurricular activities are subjectively evaluated by the selection committee through an interview process.

Timetable

Application deadline: December 1, Canadian students; April 1, international students
Notification of interview: March 15
Date interviews are held: May 1–31
Date acceptances mailed: July 7–15
Applicant's response date: August 15

Deposit (to hold place in class): none required

Deferments: are considered for extenuating circumstances.

Expenses for the 1995–96 Academic Year

Tuition and fees

Resident	$ 3,469.00 Canadian
Nonresident	
Contract students and other Canadian residents	$ 3,469.00 Canadian
International students	$30,638.00 Canadian
Living expenses (estimated)	$3,000–$5,000 Canadian

1993–94 Admissions Summary

	Number of Applicants	Number of New Entrants
In-province	18	10
Contract	106	31
Out-of-region	32	1
International	31	9
Total:	187	51

School begins: September 6, 1995; registration, September 5, 1995

Evaluation Criteria

	% *weight*
Grades	60
Animal/veterinary experience, interview, references	30
Essay	10

Western College of Veterinary Medicine
University of Saskatchewan
Saskatoon Saskatchewan S7N 0W0
Canada
Telephone: (306) 966-7452

The Western College of Veterinary Medicine is located in the city of Saskatoon, which has a population of about 180,0000 and is the major urban center in central Saskatchewan. The city is also the major commercial center for central and northern Saskatchewan and is served by two national airlines with direct connections to all major centers in Canada. Summers are short and cool; winters are long and cold.

The Western College of Veterinary Medicine is one of the few veterinary colleges where all health sciences and agriculture are offered. The college is devoted to undergraduate education and has a reputation in Canada and in the northwestern United States for educating veterinarians who are well rounded in general veterinary medicine and have good practical backgrounds. It has one of the best field service caseloads in North America.

Application Information

Applications available: September 1

Application deadline: January 4

Application fee: $35.00

Residency implications for applicants: students are selected for quota positions from Saskatchewan, Manitoba, British Columbia, Alberta, and the Northwest Territory. Occasional positions are available to other Canadian residents and residents of so-called underdeveloped countries without veterinary schools. Applicants from underdeveloped countries must take their preveterinary course work in Canada or the United States. Residents of foreign countries where veterinary schools exist are not considered.

(Veterinary Medical Colleges Application Service (VMCAS)): no participation.

Prerequisites for Admission

Course Requirements and Semester Hours

English	6
Physics	6
Biology	6

Genetics	3
Introductory chemistry	6
Organic chemistry	3
Mathematics or statistics	6
Biochemistry	6
Microbiology	3
Electives	<u>15</u>
Total:	60

Required undergraduate GPA: no definitive cut-off

Course completion deadline: prerequisite courses must be completed by the time of entry into the program.

Standardized examinations: none required

Additional Requirements and Considerations

Animal/veterinary work experience, motivation, and knowledge
Maturity
Leadership
Communication skills

Summary of Admission Procedure

The three-part admission procedure at the University of Saskatchewan consists of the following: an assessment of academic ability, a personal interview, and overall assessment of the application file.

Timetable

Application deadline: January 3
Notification of interview: May to June 5
Date interviews are held: May–June
Date acceptances mailed: July 1
Applicant's response date: maximum 10 days

Deposit (to hold place in class): none required

Deferments: not considered.

Expenses for the 1995–96 Academic Year

Tuition and fees

Resident	$3,750.00 Canadian
Nonresident	
Contract student	$3,750.00 Canadian
Other nonresident	$3,750.00 Canadian

Living expenses (estimated)

Personal (room and board)	$6,300.00 Canadian
Books, instruments, special clothing, travel	$3,400.00 Canadian
Microscope (first year)	$1,350.00 Canadian

1994–95 Admissions Summary

	Number of Applicants	*Number of New Entrants*
In-state	85	20
Contract	272	49
Out-of-state	15	1
Total:	372	70

School begins: late August

Evaluation Criteria*

	% weight
Grades	60
Animal/veterinary experience, interview	30
Judgement	10

* Interview selection is 100% grades.

Senior year veterinary students from Ohio State are shown exploring job opportunities in public health with a staff veterinarian at an Ohio meat packing plant.

PHOTO BY JOHN J. SWARTZ

137

APPLICATION AND
ENROLLMENT DATA

Table 1

Historical Summary of Applications and Applicants to United States Colleges of Veterinary Medicine, 1977–1995

Year	Number of Colleges	First-Year Positions	Number of Applications	Applications Per Position	Number of Applicants
1977	22	1973	10704	5.43	—
1978	22	2086	9467	4.54	—
1979	24	2296	10120	4.41	—
1980	25	2213	9525	4.30	7286
1981	26	2220	8367	3.65	6373
1982	26	2231	8262	3.70	6182
1983[†]	27	2306	8074	3.50	5805
1984	27	2300	8291	3.60	5503
1985	27	2282	7953	3.49	4961
1986	27	2277	7719	3.39	4751
1987	27	2199	7729	3.51	4432
1988	27	2195	7422	3.38	4200
1989	27	2189	7098	3.24	3922
1990	27	2191	7218	3.29	3955
1991	27	2172	7848	3.61	4296
1992	27	2317	8737	3.77	4709
1993	27	2309	9939	4.30	4957
1994	27	2314	10961	4.74	5428
1995	27	2290	12499	5.46	6634

[*] Assumes all spaces filled.
[†] Data for 1983 may be inconsistent due to incomplete reporting from two colleges.

Applicants Per Position	Percentage Accepted*	Applications Per Applicant	Repeat Applicants	New Applicants
—	—	—	—	—
—	—	—	—	—
—	—	—	—	—
3.29	30.40	1.31	—	—
2.87	34.80	1.31	—	—
2.77	36.10	1.34	—	—
2.52	39.80	1.39	2121	3684
2.39	41.80	1.51	1842	3661
2.17	46.00	1.60	1660	3301
2.09	47.93	1.62	1394	3357
2.02	49.62	1.74	1252	3180
1.91	52.26	1.77	1095	3105
1.79	55.81	1.81	984	2938
1.81	55.40	1.83	862	3093
1.98	50.56	1.83	861	3435
2.03	49.20	1.86	960	3749
2.15	46.58	2.01	1117	3840
2.35	42.63	2.02	1380	4048
2.89	34.40	1.88	1755	4879

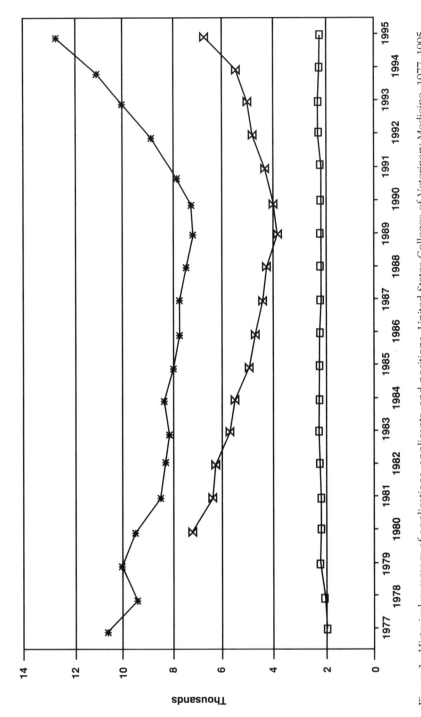

Figure 1. Historical summary of applications, applicants, and positions. United States Colleges of Veterinary Medicine, 1977–1995.
✳ = applications; ⊠ = applicants; ☐ = positions.

Table 2

Historical Summary of Applicants to United States Colleges of Veterinary Medicine by Ethnicity and Gender, 1985–1995

All Applicants

Year	Total	White	African-American	Hispanic	Native American	Asian Pacific	Ethnicity Unknown
1985	4961	4621	108	125	39	68	—
1986	4751	4419	128	132	20	52	—
1987	4432	4106	104	141	25	56	—
1988	4200	3891	110	117	23	59	—
1989	3922	3619	90	121	23	69	—
1990	3955	3639	88	122	22	84	—
1991	4296	3900	100	148	22	86	40
1992	4709	4210	109	176	43	74	97
1993	4957	4300	115	180	45	239	78
1994	5428	4775	132	184	58	229	50
1995	6634	5966	138	200	42	154	134

Male Applicants

Year	Total	White	African-American	Hispanic	Native American	Asian Pacific	Ethnicity Unknown
1985	2204	2054	52	60	19	19	—
1986	2019	1872	57	64	9	17	—
1987	1868	1717	49	69	12	21	—
1988	1689	1551	48	58	12	20	—
1989	1490	1367	30	58	11	24	—
1990	1465	1344	24	61	9	27	—
1991	1507	1349	44	67	11	27	9
1992	1613	1431	36	77	13	22	34
1993	1719	1484	37	69	13	89	27
1994	1810	1575	43	79	21	69	23
1995	2158	1931	40	70	14	54	49

Female Applicants

Year	Total	White	African-American	Hispanic	Native American	Asian Pacific	Ethnicity Unknown
1985	2757	2567	56	65	20	49	—
1986	2732	2547	71	68	11	35	—
1987	2564	2389	55	72	13	35	—
1988	2511	2340	62	59	11	39	—
1989	2432	2252	60	63	12	45	—
1990	2490	2295	64	61	13	57	—
1991	2789	2551	56	81	11	59	31
1992	3096	2779	73	99	30	52	63
1993	3238	2816	78	111	32	150	51
1994	3618	3200	89	105	37	160	27
1995	4476	4035	98	130	28	100	85

Table 3

Applicants to United States Colleges of Veterinary Medicine by Residence, 1985–1995

State	1985	1986	1987	1988	1989	1990
Alabama	85	94	115	115	117	122
Alaska	8	13	24	16	13	11
Arizona	48	35	42	50	30	35
Arkansas	39	36	36	41	26	25
California	424	419	396	421	377	353
Colorado	184	182	148	141	142	143
Connecticut	62	67	58	40	54	47
Delaware	4	8	4	7	7	7
Dist. of Col.	2	2	3	4	—	4
Florida	226	222	244	169	165	144
Georgia	109	133	135	124	109	90
Hawaii	19	9	16	15	17	21
Idaho	31	23	25	34	16	19
Illinois	227	187	143	177	149	184
Indiana	120	106	90	101	75	74
Iowa	106	97	78	80	83	110
Kansas	78	84	80	73	75	53
Kentucky	118	104	68	65	44	53
Louisiana	122	110	95	70	60	66
Maine	7	8	18	9	12	14
Maryland	104	102	98	82	90	87
Massachusetts	137	114	113	100	121	95
Michigan	183	180	206	189	151	165
Minnesota	102	100	83	68	67	79
Mississippi	89	68	71	67	67	61
Missouri	125	92	82	65	77	69
Montana	27	23	22	28	25	20
Nebraska	49	52	38	47	27	33
Nevada	10	18	17	14	25	10
New Hampshire	13	15	15	19	11	12
New Jersey	131	132	121	115	99	103

1991	1992	1993	1994	1995	% Change 85-95	% Change 94-95
116	124	129	135	153	80.0	13.3
14	17	15	11	11	37.5	0.0
51	50	59	70	101	110.4	44.3
30	30	44	30	43	10.3	43.3
409	439	386	434	545	28.5	25.6
174	203	230	274	300	63.0	9.5
50	24	46	57	94	51.6	64.9
13	9	13	9	13	225.0	44.4
—	1	—	5	7	250.0	40.0
143	176	188	197	239	5.8	21.3
112	136	134	153	194	78.0	26.8
16	16	18	18	30	57.9	66.7
27	31	31	38	46	48.4	21.1
185	209	210	233	261	15.0	12.0
91	117	111	116	133	10.8	14.7
135	81	130	95	110	3.8	15.8
66	90	88	99	91	16.7	− 8.1
71	80	97	93	97	− 17.8	4.3
81	83	93	99	114	− 6.6	15.2
16	11	16	24	54	671.4	125.0
87	105	107	156	119	14.4	− 23.7
102	106	100	153	220	60.6	43.8
149	181	140	175	209	14.2	19.4
91	96	112	104	177	73.5	70.2
60	55	37	43	50	− 51.7	16.3
78	96	91	121	132	5.6	9.1
24	24	18	31	32	18.5	3.2
41	45	48	61	60	22.4	− 1.6
14	13	16	22	22	120.0	0.0
15	24	22	20	29	123.1	45.0
106	126	94	97	112	− 14.5	15.5

Table 3 (cont.)

Applicants to United States Colleges of Veterinary Medicine by Residence, 1985–1995

State	1985	1986	1987	1988	1989	1990
New Mexico	35	37	27	23	26	21
New York	269	267	254	235	244	267
North Carolina	110	97	98	119	115	97
North Dakota	16	15	16	16	11	11
Ohio	209	209	165	193	158	198
Oklahoma	88	103	93	81	59	74
Oregon	62	61	51	48	50	45
Pennsylvania	210	192	185	159	153	155
Puerto Rico	31	32	41	27	24	35
Rhode Island	9	6	13	8	7	13
South Carolina	29	35	32	37	35	35
South Dakota	6	9	7	6	4	10
Tennessee	94	82	88	64	74	65
Texas	314	306	255	241	229	252
Utah	26	22	20	19	16	17
Vermont	12	7	7	9	17	13
Virginia	140	123	103	125	120	109
Virgin Islands	—	—	—	3	—	1
Washington	110	119	119	88	92	64
West Virginia	30	28	19	16	12	18
Wisconsin	124	109	114	95	104	96
Wyoming	10	16	12	11	9	11
United States Total	4923	4710	4403	4169	3890	3916
Foreign residence Total	38	41	29	31	32	39
Unlisted residence Total	—	—	—	—	—	—
Grand total	4961	4751	4432	4200	3922	3955
% Change from preceding year	—	−4	−7	−5	−7	1

1991	1992	1993	1994	1995	% Change 85-95	% Change 94-95
34	33	33	40	45	28.6	12.5
227	268	221	258	404	50.2	56.6
109	115	157	196	223	102.7	13.8
13	13	17	23	38	137.5	65.2
178	186	187	199	257	23.0	29.1
52	81	81	107	123	39.8	15.0
55	67	63	41	88	41.9	114.6
176	179	187	186	247	17.6	32.8
43	48	37	47	53	71.0	12.8
10	12	13	23	17	88.9	− 26.1
26	30	51	57	44	51.7	− 22.8
9	12	4	5	33	450.0	560.0
73	78	93	112	117	24.5	4.5
293	282	312	347	396	26.1	14.1
17	32	29	32	34	30.8	6.3
5	11	16	16	11	− 8.3	− 31.3
110	128	117	155	174	24.3	12.3
—	1	2	3	1	—	− 66.7
92	107	149	138	143	30.0	3.6
18	25	25	24	23	− 23.3	− 4.2
126	130	134	14	211	70.2	1407.1
14	15	16	19	23	130.0	21.1
4247	4651	4767	5215	6503	32.1	24.7
44	47	34	33	50	31.6	51.5
5	11	156	180	81	—	− 55.0
4296	4709	4957	5428	6634	33.7	22.2
9	10	5	10	33.8		

Table 4

Number of Applications per Applicant by Residence, 1995

State	Total Applicants	1	2	3	4	5	6	7	8	9	10 Plus
Alabama	153	25	17	4	2	0	0	1	0	0	0
Alaska	11	4	2	2	1	1	0	1	0	0	0
Arizona	101	32	21	25	8	4	7	2	1	0	1
Arkansas	43	22	12	6	3	0	1	0	0	0	0
California	545	264	73	54	55	38	19	14	9	4	15
Colorado	300	251	25	13	7	2	0	0	1	0	1
Connecticut	94	43	10	10	12	4	6	2	2	1	4
Delaware	13	6	2	1	1	0	0	2	1	0	0
Dist. of Col.	7	2	2	0	1	1	0	0	0	0	2
Florida	239	154	32	19	10	8	5	4	2	3	2
Georgia	194	156	25	4	2	0	3	3	1	0	0
Hawaii	30	4	5	3	5	5	4	2	1	1	0
Idaho	46	37	4	2	1	1	1	0	0	0	0
Illinois	261	167	35	26	17	7	5	1	2	0	1
Indiana	133	91	18	9	6	5	2	0	0	1	1
Iowa	110	97	9	1	1	2	0	0	0	0	0
Kansas	91	81	6	1	2	1	0	0	0	0	0
Kentucky	97	75	10	2	4	0	4	1	1	0	0
Louisianna	114	105	8	1	4	0	4	0	0	0	0
Maine	54	38	4	5	3	1	2	1	0	0	0
Maryland	119	49	23	16	12	8	6	3	0	2	0
Massachusetts	220	123	23	27	17	15	5	4	3	2	1
Michigan	209	180	12	7	2	1	2	2	1	1	1
Minnesota	177	159	15	2	0	1	0	0	0	0	0
Mississippi	50	46	2	2	0	0	0	0	0	0	0
Missouri	132	107	13	8	2	1	0	0	1	0	0
Montana	32	10	4	7	7	1	0	1	2	0	0
Nebraska	60	31	12	8	8	1	0	0	0	0	0
Nevada	22	7	3	3	3	1	2	1	0	1	1
New Hampshire	29	17	4	0	4	1	1	0	2	0	0

148

State	Total Applicants	Total Number of Applications Submitted									
		1	2	3	4	5	6	7	8	9	10 Plus
New Jersey	112	43	14	9	11	15	7	8	0	2	3
New Mexico	45	20	6	11	6	1	0	1	0	0	0
New York	404	196	58	47	30	26	15	11	13	3	5
North Carolina	223	171	26	16	7	2	0	1	0	0	0
North Dakota	38	24	7	4	2	0	1	0	0	0	0
Ohio	257	191	31	17	9	5	2	0	1	0	1
Oklahoma	123	118	4	1	0	0	0	0	0	0	0
Oregon	88	70	11	4	1	0	2	0	0	0	0
Pennsylvania	247	111	35	50	25	9	3	2	3	4	5
Puerto Rico	53	26	5	5	8	2	2	2	1	2	0
Rhode Island	17	10	1	2	0	2	0	0	1	0	0
South Carolina	44	29	4	6	2	1	0	2	0	0	0
South Dakota	33	27	5	1	0	0	0	0	0	0	0
Tennessee	117	77	19	11	3	2	2	0	2	1	0
Texas	396	362	15	12	0	4	1	2	0	0	0
Utah	34	6	11	7	6	4	0	0	0	0	0
Vermont	11	6	2	0	2	1	0	0	0	0	0
Virginia	174	104	28	14	10	10	4	2	0	2	0
Virgin Islands	1	0	0	0	1	0	0	0	0	0	0
Washington	143	118	13	4	4	0	0	2	1	0	1
West Virginia	23	8	9	2	1	2	1	0	0	0	0
Wisconsin	211	170	29	6	2	2	2	0	0	0	0
Wyoming	23	11	3	1	6	1	0	0	0	1	0
United States Total	6503	4385	766	498	332	199	119	78	52	32	45
Foreign residence Total	50	40	4	0	3	0	0	0	1	0	0
Unlisted residence Total	81	25	17	17	11	4	1	0	3	2	1
Grand Total	6634	4450	787	515	346	203	120	78	56	34	46

Table 5

Applications per Position in Entering Class in United States Colleges of Veterinary Medicine, 1990-1995

College	1990			1991			1992		
	A	P	A/P	A	P	A/P	A	P	A/P
Auburn Univ	223	90	2.48	245	91	2.69	328	90	3.64
Univ of California	395	122	3.24	440	122	3.61	495	122	4.06
Colorado State	327	125	2.62	408	131	3.11	460	130	3.54
Cornell Univ	447	80	5.59	442	81	5.46	437	80	5.46
Univ of Florida	271	80	3.39	238	79	3.01	318	82	3.88
Univ of Georgia	216	80	2.70	204	79	2.58	269	80	3.36
Univ of Illinois	292	80	3.65	266	81	3.28	271	100	2.71
Iowa State	316	76	4.16	356	79	4.51	131	100	1.31
Kansas State	129	100	1.29	211	83	2.54	265	100	2.65
Louisiana State	149	66	2.26	226	67	3.37	256	73	3.51
Michigan State	447	100	4.47	462	115	4.02	509	100	5.09
Univ of Minnesota	248	68	3.65	302	72	4.19	424	76	5.58
Mississippi State	150	45	3.33	186	45	4.13	146	50	2.92
Univ of Missouri	150	64	2.34	180	64	2.81	223	64	3.48
North Carolina State	188	72	2.61	215	72	2.99	256	72	3.56
Ohio State	366	130	2.82	338	129	2.62	328	130	2.52
Oklahoma State	141	70	2.01	125	70	1.79	223	71	3.14
Oregon State	170	36	4.72	158	36	4.39	188	37	5.08
Univ of Pennsylvania	550	109	5.05	532	111	4.79	559	111	5.04
Purdue Univ	289	60	4.82	303	63	4.81	390	62	6.29
Univ of Tennessee	179	60	2.98	210	58	3.62	219	62	3.53
Texas A&M	248	128	1.94	291	115	2.53	311	128	2.43
Tufts Univ	319	70	4.56	373	73	5.11	379	75	5.05
Tuskegee Univ	149	60	2.48	151	41	3.68	203	60	3.38
VA-MD Regional	181	80	2.26	182	75	2.43	206	82	2.51
Washington State	305	60	5.08	371	60	6.18	458	100	4.58
Univ of Wisconin	373	80	4.66	433	80	5.41	485	80	6.06
Total	7218	2191	3.29	7848	2172	3.61	8737	2317	3.77

A = total applications; P = positions in entering class as reported in this survey; A/P = applications received per position in the entering class.

150

	1993			1994			1995	
A	P	A/P	A	P	A/P	A	P	A/P
376	92	4.09	415	90	4.61	446	92	4.85
459	122	3.76	471	108	4.36	552	108	5.11
519	133	3.90	656	133	4.93	764	132	5.79
437	82	5.33	522	82	6.37	622	82	7.59
357	79	4.52	384	79	4.86	487	80	6.09
336	80	4.20	381	80	4.76	431	87	4.95
288	86	3.35	361	86	4.20	379	87	4.36
536	100	5.36	590	100	5.90	690	100	6.90
259	108	2.40	331	100	3.31	341	107	3.19
310	72	4.31	296	77	3.84	371	80	4.64
515	101	5.10	540	100	5.40	554	100	5.54
482	76	6.34	504	76	6.63	489	76	6.43
120	49	2.45	84	49	1.71	167	49	3.41
198	64	3.09	236	64	3.69	295	64	4.61
388	73	5.32	452	73	6.19	500	78	6.41
330	128	2.58	342	128	2.67	423	133	3.18
272	70	3.89	318	70	4.54	411	71	5.79
195	35	5.57	232	34	6.82	324	36	9.00
587	111	5.29	559	130	4.30	744	109	6.83
444	64	6.94	386	67	5.76	506	69	7.33
285	65	4.38	334	65	5.14	334	63	5.30
398	128	3.11	431	128	3.37	431	128	3.37
429	71	6.04	581	75	7.75	685	75	9.13
236	60	3.93	232	62	3.74	208	62	3.35
201	83	2.42	201	80	2.51	249	80	3.11
442	97	4.56	560	98	5.71	502	62	8.10
540	80	6.75	562	80	7.03	594	80	7.43
9939	2309	4.30	10961	2314	4.74	12499	2290	5.46

Table 6

A Comparison of Applicants to United States Medical and Veterinary Colleges by Gender and Ethnicity, 1984–1994

*Medical Schools**

| Class | Number of Applicants | | | Total | | Number Enrolled | | |
Entering	Male	Female	Total	Applications	A/A[†]	Male	Female	Total
1984	23,468	12,486	35,954	331,937	9.23	10,926	5,469	16,395
1985	21,331	11,562	32,893	307,427	9.35	10,748	5,520	18,268
1986	20,056	11,267	31,323	295,744	9.44	10,529	5,574	18,103
1987	17,712	10,411	28,123	266,900	9.49	10,160	5,767	15,927
1988	16,457	10,264	26,721	258,442	9.67	10,091	5,878	15,969
1989	16,369	10,546	26,915	262,476	9.75	9,842	6,025	15,867
1990	17,458	11,785	28,243	290,489	9.93	9,845	6,153	15,998
1991	19,601	13,700	33,301	354,017	10.63	9,778	6,433	16,211
1992	21,791	15,619	37,410	405,720	10.85	9,517	6,772	16,289
1993	24,851	17,957	42,808	482,788	11.28	10,074	7,288	17,362
1994	26,397	18,968	45,365	561,593	12.38	9,468	6,819	16,287

Veterinary Schools

| Class | Number of Applicants | | | Total | | Number Enrolled | | |
Entering	Male	Female	Total	Applications	A/A	Male	Female	Total
1984	2,621	2,882	5,503	8,291	1.51	1,153	1,176	2,329
1985	2,204	2,757	4,961	7,953	1.60	1,015	1,265	2,280
1986	2,019	2,732	4,751	7,719	1.62	945	1,330	2,275
1987	1,868	2,564	4,432	7,729	1.74	943	1,264	2,207
1988	1,689	2,511	4,200	7,422	1.77	902	1,292	2,194
1989	1,490	2,432	3,922	7,098	1.81	821	1,393	2,214
1990	1,465	2,490	3,955	7,218	1.83	844	1,353	2,197
1991	1,507	2,789	4,296	7,848	1.83	786	1,439	2,225
1992	1,613	3,096	4,709	8,737	1.86	768	1,491	2,259
1993	1,719	3,238	4,957	9,939	2.01	824	1,472	2,296
1994	1,810	3,618	5,428	10,961	2.02	774	1,502	2,276

* Data obtained from the Association of American Medical Colleges, Washington, DC.

[†] A/A = applications per applicant.

[‡] The percentage of men and women enrolled of the total number of male and female applicants, respectively.

% Enrolled[‡]		Applicants		Entering Class		Minorities as % of All Applicants			
Male	Female	M:F	%F	M:F	%F	African-American	Hispanic	Native American	Asian Pacific
46.6	43.8	1.88	34.7	2.00	33.4	7.4	2.3	0.4	—
50.4	47.7	1.84	35.2	1.95	33.9	7.4	2.4	0.4	—
52.5	49.5	1.78	36.0	1.89	34.6	7.6	2.2	0.4	—
57.4	55.4	1.70	37.0	1.76	36.2	7.8	2.4	0.4	—
61.3	57.3	1.60	38.4	1.72	36.8	8.1	2.3	0.4	—
60.1	57.1	1.55	39.2	1.63	38.0	8.2	2.5	0.5	—
56.4	52.2	1.48	40.3	1.60	38.5	8.1	5.8	0.5	—
49.9	47.0	1.43	41.1	1.52	39.9	8.0	5.8	0.5	16.5
43.7	43.4	1.40	41.8	1.41	41.6	7.8	5.8	0.5	16.6
40.5	40.6	1.38	41.9	1.38	42.0	8.2	5.4	0.6	18.3
35.9	36.0	1.39	41.8	1.39	41.9	8.1	5.6	0.6	19.4

% Enrolled		Applicants		Entering Class		Minorities as % of All Applicants			
Male	Female	M:F	%F	M:F	%F	African-American	Hispanic	Native American	Asian Pacific
44.0	40.8	0.91	52.4	0.98	50.5	2.0	2.3	0.6	1.2
46.1	45.9	0.80	55.8	0.80	55.5	2.2	2.5	0.8	1.4
46.8	48.7	0.74	57.5	0.71	58.5	2.6	2.5	0.4	1.1
50.5	49.3	0.73	57.9	0.75	57.3	2.3	3.2	0.6	1.3
53.4	51.5	0.67	59.8	0.70	58.9	2.6	2.8	0.5	1.4
55.1	57.3	0.61	62.0	0.59	62.9	2.3	3.1	0.6	1.8
57.6	54.3	0.59	63.0	0.62	61.6	2.2	3.1	0.6	2.1
52.2	51.6	0.54	64.9	0.55	64.7	2.3	3.4	0.5	2.0
47.6	48.2	0.52	65.7	0.52	66.0	2.3	3.7	0.9	1.6
47.9	45.5	0.53	65.3	0.56	64.1	2.3	3.6	0.9	4.8
42.8	41.5	0.50	68.7	0.52	66.0	2.4	3.4	1.1	4.2

Table 7

Success* of First-Time and Repeat Applicants, 1990–1995

	1990			1991			1992		
	Total	Accepted		Total	Accepted		Total	Accepted	
Applicants	Appl.	#	%	Appl.	#	%	Appl.	#	%
First-time	3093	1804	58.3	3435	1827	53.2	3749	1825	48.7
Repeat	862	445	51.6	861	392	45.5	960	426	44.4
Total	3955	2249	56.9	4296	2219	51.7	4709	2251	47.8

* Success indicates the receipt by an applicant of one or more offers of admission on or before June 15.

Table 8

Success* of Applicants by Ethnicity, 1990–1995

		1990			1991		
		Total	Accepted		Total	Accepted	
Applicants		Appl.	#	%	Appl.	#	%
White	First-time	808	416	51.5	786	359	45.7
	Repeat	2831	1673	59.1	3114	1685	54.1
	Total	3639	2089	57.4	3900	2044	52.4
African–American	First-time	11	7	63.6	14	7	50.0
	Repeat	77	39	50.6	86	41	47.7
	Total	88	46	52.3	100	48	48.0
Hispanic	First-time	25	17	68.0	28	9	34.6
	Repeat	97	51	52.6	122	47	38.5
	Total	122	68	55.7	148	56	37.8
Asian Pacific	First-time	14	4	28.6	21	9	42.9
	Repeat	70	31	44.3	65	35	53.8
	Total	84	35	41.7	86	44	51.2
Native American	First-time	4	1	25.0	2	2	100.0
	Repeat	18	10	55.6	20	7	35.0
	Total	22	11	50.0	22	9	40.9
Other	First-time	—	—	—	12	6	50.0
	Repeat	—	—	—	28	12	42.9
	Total	—	—	—	40	18	45.0
Total	First-time	862	445	51.6	861	392	45.5
	Repeat	3093	1804	58.3	3435	1827	53.2
	Total	3955	2249	56.9	4296	2219	51.7

* Success indicates the receipt by an applicant of one or more offers of admission on or before June 15.

	1993			1994			1995	
Total Appl.	Accepted #	%	Total Appl.	Accepted #	%	Total Appl.	Accepted #	%
3840	1774	46.2	4048	1828	45.2	4879	1714	35.1
1117	427	38.2	1380	565	40.9	1755	566	32.3
4957	2201	44.4	5428	2393	44.1	6634	2280	34.4

	1992			1993			1994			1995	
Total Appl.	Accepted #	%	Total Appl.	Accepted #	%	Total Appl.	Accepted #	%	Total Appl.	Accepted #	%
849	377	44.4	940	370	39.4	1206	505	41.9	1596	523	32.8
3361	1650	49.1	3360	1560	46.4	3569	1638	45.9	4370	1576	36.1
4210	2027	48.1	4300	1930	44.9	4775	2143	44.9	5966	2099	35.2
20	8	40.0	30	9	30.0	34	8	23.5	30	7	23.3
89	37	41.6	85	43	50.6	98	31	31.6	108	29	26.9
109	45	41.3	115	52	45.2	132	39	29.5	138	36	26.1
45	24	53.3	39	9	23.1	40	17	42.5	55	19	34.5
131	56	42.7	141	61	43.3	144	60	41.7	145	30	20.7
176	80	45.5	180	70	38.9	184	77	41.8	200	49	24.5
13	8	61.5	75	28	37.3	66	23	34.6	22	7	31.8
61	31	50.8	164	70	42.7	163	71	43.6	132	39	29.5
74	39	52.7	239	98	41.0	229	94	41.0	154	46	29.9
12	3	25.0	13	3	23.1	17	4	23.5	17	3	17.6
31	13	41.9	32	13	40.6	41	17	41.5	25	7	28.0
43	16	37.2	45	16	35.6	58	21	36.2	42	10	23.8
21	6	28.6	20	8	40.0	17	8	47.1	35	7	20.0
76	38	50.0	58	27	46.6	33	11	33.3	99	33	33.3
97	44	45.4	78	35	44.9	50	19	38.0	134	40	29.9
960	426	44.4	1117	427	38.2	1380	565	40.9	1755	566	32.3
3749	1825	48.7	3840	1774	46.2	4048	1828	45.2	4879	1714	35.1
4709	2251	47.8	4957	2201	44.4	5428	2393	44.1	6634	2280	34.4

Table 9

Success* of Applicants by Age, 1990–1995

		1990			1991		
		Total	Accepted		Total	Accepted	
Age	Applicants	Appl.	#	%	Appl.	#	%
<20	First-time	—	—	—	1	0	0.0
	Repeat	5	3	60.0	23	13	58.5
	Total	5	3	60.0	24	13	54.2
20–24	First-time	425	226	53.2	464	222	47.8
	Repeat	2027	1240	61.2	2170	1215	56.0
	Total	2452	1466	59.8	2634	1437	54.6
25–29	First-time	299	143	47.8	271	114	42.1
	Repeat	643	330	51.3	732	330	45.1
	Total	942	473	50.2	1003	444	44.3
30–34	First-time	90	48	53.3	78	32	41.0
	Repeat	272	150	55.1	301	159	52.8
	Total	362	198	54.7	379	191	50.4
35–39	First-time	38	26	68.4	32	16	50.0
	Repeat	107	59	55.1	152	85	55.9
	Total	145	85	58.6	184	101	54.9
>39	First-time	10	2	20.0	15	8	53.3
	Repeat	39	23	59.0	57	25	43.9
	Total	49	25	51.0	72	33	45.8
Total	First-time	862	445	51.6	861	392	45.5
	Repeat	3093	1805	58.4	3435	1827	53.2
	Total	3955	2250	56.9	4296	2219	51.7

* Success indicates the receipt by an applicant of one or more offers of admission on or before June 15.

	1992			1993			1994			1995	
Total Appl.	Accepted #	%	Total Appl.	Accepted #	%	Total Appl.	Accepted #	%	Total Appl.	Accepted #	%
—	—	0.0	—	—	0.0	—	—	0.0	—	—	0.0
6	4	68.7	1	1	100.0	9	3	33.3	9	4	44.4
6	4	68.7	1	1	100.0	9	3	33.3	9	4	44.4
503	233	46.3	598	231	38.6	744	313	42.1	880	308	35.0
2465	1235	50.1	2490	1184	47.6	2571	1223	47.6	2781	1077	38.7
2968	1468	49.5	3088	1415	45.8	3315	1536	46.3	3661	1385	37.8
280	110	39.3	328	118	36.0	421	161	38.2	582	150	25.8
788	361	45.8	810	347	42.8	885	348	39.3	1004	334	33.3
1068	471	44.1	1138	465	40.9	1306	509	39.0	1586	484	30.5
96	46	47.9	112	47	42.0	130	59	45.4	173	61	35.3
284	128	45.1	321	136	42.4	355	146	41.1	348	138	39.7
380	174	45.8	433	183	42.3	485	205	42.3	521	199	38.2
60	28	48.7	52	22	42.3	51	22	43.1	69	26	37.7
133	66	49.6	155	75	48.4	152	71	46.7	147	56	38.1
193	94	48.7	207	97	46.9	203	93	45.8	216	82	38.0
21	9	42.9	27	9	33.3	34	10	29.4	50	21	42.0
73	31	42.5	63	31	49.2	76	37	48.7	104	33	31.7
94	40	42.6	90	40	44.4	110	47	42.7	154	54	35.1
960	426	44.4	1117	427	38.2	1380	565	40.9	1755	566	32.3
3749	1825	48.7	3840	1774	46.2	4048	1828	45.2	4879	1714	35.1
4709	2251	47.8	4957	2201	44.4	5428	2393	44.1	6634	2280	34.4

Table 10

Success* of Applicants by Residence, 1990–1995

State	1990 Total Appl.	1990 Accepted #	1990 Accepted %	1991 Total Appl.	1991 Accepted #	1991 Accepted %
Alabama	122	52	42.6	116	51	44.0
Alaska	11	8	72.7	14	5	35.7
Arizona	35	19	54.3	51	27	52.9
Arkansas	25	19	76.0	30	22	73.3
California	353	159	45.0	409	171	41.8
Colorado	143	64	44.8	174	68	44.8
Connecticut	47	26	55.3	50	31	62.0
Delaware	7	5	71.4	13	7	53.8
Dist. of Col.	4	1	25.0	—	—	0.0
Florida	144	83	57.6	143	76	53.1
Georgia	90	56	62.2	112	50	44.6
Hawaii	21	10	47.6	16	6	37.5
Idaho	19	12	63.2	27	15	55.6
Illinois	184	93	50.5	185	98	53.0
Indiana	74	37	50.0	91	40	44.0
Iowa	110	76	69.1	135	62	45.9
Kansas	53	46	86.8	66	45	68.2
Kentucky	53	39	73.6	71	38	53.5
Louisiana	66	49	74.2	81	50	61.7
Maine	14	7	50.0	16	3	18.8
Maryland	87	51	58.6	87	51	58.6
Massachusetts	95	52	54.7	102	59	57.8
Michigan	165	87	52.7	149	74	49.7
Minnesota	79	55	69.6	91	47	51.6
Mississippi	61	33	54.1	60	33	55.0
Missouri	69	53	76.8	78	52	66.7
Montana	20	12	60.0	24	13	54.2
Nebraska	33	27	81.8	41	34	82.9
Nevada	10	7	70.0	14	8	57.1

	1992			1993			1994			1995		
	Total Appl.	Accepted #	Accepted %	Total Appl.	Accepted #	Accepted %	Total Appl.	Accepted #	Accepted %	Total Appl.	Accepted #	Accepted %
	124	56	45.2	129	55	42.6	135	57	42.2	153	50	32.7
	17	5	29.4	15	3	20.0	11	6	54.5	11	4	36.4
	50	23	46.0	59	22	37.3	70	22	31.4	101	28	27.7
	30	21	70.0	44	21	47.7	30	12	40.0	43	10	23.3
	439	187	42.6	386	167	43.3	434	187	43.1	545	164	30.1
	203	69	34.0	230	66	28.7	274	73	26.6	300	66	22.0
	24	7	29.2	46	19	41.3	57	26	45.6	94	21	22.3
	9	4	44.4	13	7	53.8	9	3	33.3	13	3	23.1
	1	0	0.0	—	—	0.0	55	1	20.0	7	2	28.6
	176	81	46.0	188	84	44.7	197	96	48.7	239	89	37.2
	136	68	50.0	134	66	49.3	153	55	35.9	194	55	28.4
	16	8	50.0	18	6	33.3	18	8	44.4	30	12	40.0
	31	14	45.2	31	11	35.5	38	15	47.4	46	16	34.8
	209	84	40.2	210	84	40.0	233	100	42.9	261	85	32.6
	117	44	37.6	111	40	38.0	116	45	38.8	133	46	34.6
	81	60	74.1	130	58	44.6	95	71	74.7	110	62	56.4
	90	52	57.8	88	49	55.7	99	52	52.5	91	49	53.8
	80	45	56.3	97	40	41.2	93	48	51.6	97	32	33.0
	83	49	59.0	93	54	58.1	99	60	60.6	114	58	50.9
	11	6	54.5	16	6	37.5	24	11	45.8	54	13	24.1
	105	49	46.7	107	49	45.8	156	65	41.7	119	49	41.2
	106	48	45.3	100	32	32.0	153	65	42.5	220	78	35.5
	181	74	40.9	140	71	50.7	175	81	46.3	209	76	36.4
	96	53	55.2	112	60	53.6	104	54	51.9	177	62	35.0
	55	27	49.1	37	29	78.4	43	33	76.7	50	26	52.0
	96	60	62.5	91	50	54.9	121	58	47.9	132	62	47.0
	24	11	45.8	18	10	55.6	31	8	25.8	32	7	21.9
	45	28	62.2	48	19	39.6	61	34	55.7	60	30	50.0
	13	8	61.5	16	5	31.3	22	6	27.3	22	6	27.3

Table 10 (cont.)

Success* of Applicants by Residence, 1990–1995

State	1990			1991		
	Total Appl.	Accepted		Total Appl.	Accepted	
		#	%		#	%
New Hampshire	12	8	66.7	15	11	73.3
New Jersey	103	46	44.7	106	49	46.2
New Mexico	21	20	95.2	34	20	58.8
New York	267	127	47.6	227	92	40.5
North Carolina	97	66	68.0	109	62	56.9
North Dakota	11	5	45.5	13	10	76.9
Ohio	198	109	55.1	178	110	61.8
Oklahoma	74	58	78.4	52	50	96.2
Oregon	45	30	66.7	55	32	58.2
Pennsylvania	155	94	60.6	176	83	47.2
Puerto Rico	35	14	40.0	43	14	32.6
Rhode Island	13	4	30.8	10	5	50.0
South Carolina	35	23	65.7	26	16	61.5
South Dakota	10	9	90.0	9	8	88.9
Tennessee	65	43	66.2	73	45	61.6
Texas	252	133	52.8	293	144	49.1
Utah	17	13	76.5	17	11	64.7
Vermont	13	8	61.5	5	3	60.0
Virginia	109	62	56.9	110	62	56.4
Virgin Islands	1	—	0.0	—	—	0.0
Washington	64	34	53.1	92	39	42.4
West Virginia	18	13	72.2	18	13	72.2
Wisconsin	96	64	66.7	126	78	61.9
Wyoming	11	9	81.8	14	11	78.6
United States	3916	2231	57.0	4247	2204	51.9
Foreign residence	39	19	48.7	44	14	31.8
Unlisted residence	—	—	0.0	5	1	20.0
Grand total	3955	2250	56.9	4296	2219	51.7

* Success indicates the receipt by an applicant of one or more offers of admission on or before June 15.

1992			1993			1994			1995		
Total Appl.	Accepted #	%	Total Appl.	Accepted #	%	Total Appl.	Accepted #	%	Total Appl.	Accepted #	%
24	12	50.0	22	12	54.5	20	11	55.0	29	4	13.8
126	61	48.4	94	42	44.7	97	40	41.2	112	31	27.7
33	21	63.6	33	18	54.5	40	19	47.5	45	22	48.9
268	119	44.4	221	110	49.8	258	127	49.2	404	113	28.0
115	75	65.2	157	76	48.4	196	71	36.2	223	78	35.0
13	9	69.2	17	7	41.2	23	15	65.2	38	14	36.8
186	114	61.3	187	99	52.9	199	107	53.8	257	102	39.7
81	59	72.8	81	62	76.5	107	69	64.5	123	58	47.2
67	25	37.3	63	7	11.1	41	18	43.9	88	29	33.0
179	91	50.8	187	97	51.9	186	93	50.0	247	95	38.5
48	14	29.2	37	9	24.3	47	16	34.0	53	7	13.2
12	6	50.0	13	6	46.2	23	11	47.8	17	4	23.5
30	17	56.7	51	28	54.9	57	26	45.6	44	17	38.6
12	5	41.7	4	4	100.0	5	3	60.0	33	15	45.5
78	42	53.8	93	49	52.7	112	60	53.6	117	53	45.3
282	110	39.0	312	117	37.5	347	112	32.3	396	118	29.8
32	13	40.6	29	14	48.3	32	12	37.5	34	9	26.5
11	5	45.5	16	11	68.8	16	6	37.5	11	4	36.4
128	67	52.3	117	60	51.3	155	74	47.7	174	63	36.2
1	0	0.0	2	1	50.0	3	1	33.3	1	0	0.0
107	34	31.8	149	48	32.2	138	43	31.2	143	55	38.5
25	12	48.0	25	12	48.0	24	11	45.8	23	10	43.5
130	67	51.5	134	50	37.3	14	11	78.6	211	79	37.4
15	11	73.3	16	10	62.5	19	9	47.4	23	7	30.4
4651	2230	47.8	4767	2132	44.7	5215	2320	44.5	6503	2248	34.6
47	11	23.4	34	5	14.7	33	5	15.2	50	15	30.0
11	10	90.9	156	64	41.0	180	68	37.8	81	17	21.0
4709	2251	47.8	4957	2201	44.4	5428	2393	44.1	6634	2280	34.4

Table 11

Success* of Applicants with Multiple Applications, 1990–1995

Number of Applications Submitted	1990 Total Appl.	Accepted #	Accepted %	1991 Total Appl.	Accepted #	Accepted %
1	1469	1256	85.5	2968	1447	48.8
2	249	199	79.9	449	225	50.1
3	170	112	65.9	327	194	59.3
4	150	54	36.0	240	152	63.3
5	88	37	42.0	126	82	65.1
6	51	18	35.3	79	47	59.5
7	31	11	35.5	33	24	72.7
8	12	8	66.7	32	21	65.5
9	14	3	21.4	15	7	48.7
10	5	2	40.0	8	6	75.0
>10	11	5	45.5	19	14	73.7
Total	2250	1705	50.34	4296	2219	51.7

* Success indicates the receipt by an applicant of one or more offers of admission on or before June 15.

Table 12

Success* of Applicants with Multiple Applications, 1990–1995

Number of Applications Submitted	Number of Applicants	Percentage of Applicants	Total Number of Offers Received by June 15 0	1	2	3	4	5	>6
1	4450	67.08	3072	1378	0	0	0	0	0
2	787	11.86	509	222	56	0	0	0	0
3	515	7.76	304	147	48	16	0	0	0
4	346	5.22	182	108	34	19	3	0	0
5	203	3.06	118	52	13	15	3	2	0
6	120	1.81	64	27	16	8	4	1	0
7	78	1.18	37	28	5	3	4	1	0
8	56	0.84	24	15	6	8	2	1	0
9	34	0.51	15	10	2	3	2	1	2
10	24	0.36	15	5	3	1	0	0	0
11	9	0.14	6	1	2	0	0	0	0
12	5	0.08	3	0	0	1	0	1	0
13	3	0.05	2	1	0	0	0	0	0
14	2	0.03	2	0	0	0	0	0	0
18	1	0.02	1	0	0	0	0	0	0
20	1	0.02	0	0	0	0	1	0	0
Total	6834	100.00	4354	1994	185	74	19	7	2

* Success indicates the receipt by an applicant of one or more offers of admission on or before June 15.

1992			1993			1994			1995		
Total Appl.	Accepted		Total Appl.	Accepted		Total Appl.	Accepted		Total Appl.	Accepted	
	#	%		#	%		#	%		#	%
3213	1417	44.1	3222	1308	40.6	3500	1392	39.8	4450	1378	31.0
543	273	50.3	552	258	48.7	626	270	43.1	787	278	35.3
366	211	57.7	438	231	52.7	472	229	48.5	515	211	41.0
246	141	57.3	274	133	48.5	314	166	52.9	346	164	47.4
116	69	59.5	175	99	56.6	201	110	54.7	203	85	41.9
78	50	64.1	109	59	54.1	115	80	69.6	120	56	46.7
53	35	66.0	67	41	61.2	59	42	71.2	78	41	52.6
37	19	51.4	38	23	60.5	53	39	73.6	56	32	57.1
18	11	61.1	27	22	81.5	26	21	80.8	34	19	55.9
8	4	50.0	20	9	45.0	17	14	82.4	24	9	37.5
31	21	67.7	35	18	51.4	45	30	66.7	22	7	31.8
4709	2251	47.8	4957	2201	44.4	5428	2393	44.1	6634	2280	34.4